Praise for 60 Years Young with Itsy!

"Coach, marketing pro, tai-chi instructor, and family man – Itsy Lieberman has had more lives than a cat. He's seen it all and done it all. Now he tells it all – in his own inimitable way. Fasten your seatbelts for a fun ride." **Kyle Vanden Bosch—NFL All Pro Football Player, Captain Detroit Lions**

"Itsy is his own man, father, coach, super-human being. It all comes out in this book. Everyone should read. I am proud to call him my brother." **Jack L. Gilardi—Executive Vice President ICM | International Creative Management**

"Itsy's dad was good friends with my dad, Rabbi Irwin Groner, so I've known Itsy all my life. He's always been very giving to people – whether it's his time, his knowledge or his money. It's my privilege to know him and I heartily recommend his book." **David Groner—Wayne County Circuit Judge**

"The definition of an 'Itsy': a pint sized barrel chested dynamo who threw a football and a javelin a country mile. As a coach and corporate executive, he separated himself by positively influencing the lives of countless student athletes and employees. When he stands on his accomplishments, he is anything but 'Itsy". In my book, he is ten feet tall!" **Larry Sherman—Attorney, Madison Heights City Attorney, West Bloomfield Prosecuting Attorney and Member of the Michigan Jewish Sports Hall of Fame Class of 2010**

"It doesn't matter if you are young or old, rich or poor; Itsy has something to offer you. Whether it's words of wisdom, a pat on the back, a chuckle – your day will be brighter if Itsy's part of it." **Willie Horton—Former Detroit Tiger/ Baseball Legend**

"Ever wonder what goes on behind closed doors at the Big Three – or in the club house? Itsy Lieberman shares his rollicking stories of life and times in corporate America. It's a peek into a world that many of us never get to see, involving people we only know from the headlines." **Mark Hogan—Toyota Worldwide Board Member**

"Sports are like life. No one knows that better than Itsy Lieberman, a former athlete and coach who used his sports know-how to become successful in corporate America. Read this book and apply his r
ladder. You'll even have fun doing it." **Jo**
Famer

"Erwin 'Itsy' Lieberman became the Top Incentive and Recognition Marketing Person through perseverance, creativity and a dynamic and charismatic personality. As a supplier to Ford Motor Company, he was the 'go–to' person for any incentive or recognition related product, regardless of the size the timetable or the level of difficulty. Erwin is a true American success story...an athletic coach, a teacher, a successful marketer, entrepreneur, author and Sunrise-Chi instructor for senior citizens." **Jim Gwaltney—Executive, Ford Motor Company (retired); Author, "The 20 Immutable Laws of Leadership"; President, J. Gwaltney & Associates**

"With Itsy, you'll learn life's most important lesson: 'Learn to live and laugh, thus delay your epitaph.'" **Marty Seltzer—Managing Director, Chester Street Assisted Living Community**

"When one understands the true phases of life (learn, rear and return) one will better understand the brilliance, integrity and humanitarianism of Ervin 'Itsy' Lieberman, a true man among men." **Dr. Delbert Gray—President / Executive Director Willie Horton Foundation**

"I couldn't have asked for a better coach for my kids than Itsy. My son learned more on the playing field with Itsy than he ever learned in the classroom, which is saying a lot. Now that I've read his story '60 Years Young with Itsy' I know why." **Tony Versaci—Burger King franchisee and Former Football Coach Devine High School**

"Few people match Itsy's passion and enthusiasm for helping others."60 Years Young with Itsy" gives you an engaging glimpse into the unique journey of an extraordinary gem of a human being. Itsy shares solid, priceless, down-to-earth guidance you would expect from a friend and trusted mentor." **Al Horton— Music Industry Veteran, Former Professional Sports Agent, and Entrepreneur**

"Of all the writing projects I've ever had, working with Itsy has easily been the most fun and the most rewarding. I've met lots of people but I have never, ever met anyone quite like him—smart, funny, genuine, charming—and most of all generous. I've learned so much from him and consider it a privilege to introduce the world to him." **Laura Brestovansky—Writer**

"I just finished '60 Years Young with Itsy' and don't know which part I enjoyed more—the stories that I remembered or those from other parts of his diverse life. One thing's for sure, I clearly heard the Itsy I know on every page." **Cecilia Morey—Personal Banker, Huntington Bank**

"When most people think of 'success' they think of financial and professional success. However, success can also take the form of joy and personal relationships. Itsy is one of those rare people who has had all those forms of success and more. Let him show you how he did it." **Shirley Foon Wiss—Former widow of Alvin Foon, Founding Member of Michigan Jewish Sports Hall of Fame**

"I enthusiastically recommend '60 Years Young with Itsy.' It is the story of a man who has lived the most varied life I know—from a struggling childhood to corporate success and beyond. You can't help but be entertained by Itsy's humor, passion and joy for life." **Hajj Flemings—Founder, Brand Camp University**

"When I first met Itsy, I was still working in broadcasting and training. Like everyone else, I fell under the spell of his charisma. Watching his success in the business world made me want to learn his secrets. He has been my mentor and dear friend - and I am grateful to have some of his success rubbing off on me. Read '60 Years Young with Itsy' and it will rub off on you too!" **Sonna Johns—Account Executive, FMReps**

"Itsy has done more for me than anyone else in my life. He's my mentor and my rock and always will be." **Jami Fresch—Internet marketer**

DEDICATION

I dedicate this book to my parents, Ida and Sam Lieberman, as well as to Sam Young, Chuck Daly, and my cousin Morrie Fenkell. If it wasn't for these people being so helpful to me and sticking with me through thick and thin, I never would have had the opportunity to have had such a great career and life.

♦ ♦ ♦

TO ELIZABETH

A GREAT LADY-

LIVE YOUNG

Itsy

CHARITABLE DONATIONS

Erwin "Itsy" Lieberman will donate proceeds from the sale of this book to various charities.

60
YEARS
YOUNG
WITH

Itsy

Life Lessons from
the Locker Room,
the Board Room,
the Workout Room,
and the Family Room

ERWIN "ITSY" LIEBERMAN

Foreword by Martin "Hoot" McInerney

As told to Laura K. Brestovansky

LIEBERMAN, INC.
Royal Oak, Michigan

Lieberman, Inc.

P.O. Box 519
Royal Oak, Michigan 48068-0519   *www.60YearsYoungwithItsy.com*

Printed in the United States of America

Lieberman, Erwin L.
    60 Years Young with Itsy / Erwin L. Lieberman

ISBN 978-0-9856184-0-7

►ATTENTION ORGANIZATIONS◄

Quantity discounts of this book are available on bulk purchases for reselling, educational purposes, subscriptions or membership incentives, gifts or fundraising. Special books or book excerpts can also be created to fit specific needs. For more information, please contact:
Lieberman, Inc., P.O. Box 519, Royal Oak, MI 48068-0519
AHorton23@Yahoo.com

CONTENTS

FOREWORD

By "Hoot" McInerney

I've been privileged to have made many friends in my life. Many are famous and most are not. I'm honored to count such luminaries as the late Pope John Paul II, the late Bob Hope, Ford Motor Company Chairman William Clay Ford, and even former U.S. Presidents George H.W. Bush and Bill Clinton as my friends. I don't say this to brag (I'm not a name-dropper), but to show you where my long career has taken me, the son of immigrants.

I'm grateful for all I have received in my life and I've spent a lifetime in "paying it forward" – giving a helping hand to people. I consider it a privilege to do so.

Perhaps that's why I'm so happy to count Itsy Lieberman among my friends.

"But wait," you are probably asking, "Who is Itsy Lieberman?"

Itsy is my one of my best friends. He's one of those rare individuals who really did come from small beginnings to really make something of himself – much like I did. He's met countless celebrities, who all love him. But Itsy never brags about the people he's met. Instead he's committed to using his experiences to help others.

That's just one of the many similarities between Itsy and me.

Like me, Itsy has an unusual nickname.

Like me, Itsy came up from humble roots, knowing how important it is to have a job, any job. While I learned the automobile dealership business literally from the ground up, Itsy used his athletic ability to build a successful career as a coach. He built some fantastic high school teams, where they still talk about him today.

One career is enough for most people but Itsy managed to go even further, becoming a legend in automotive marketing. I think his coaching career taught him the people skills needed in marketing. Itsy knows how to build teams. He encourages them to work hard and, as he is so fond of saying, "stay in their lane." Don't worry about what the other guy is doing – focus on your own job.

Like me, Itsy recognizes the importance of family. I have several family members working with me in my dealerships, including my brother and my son. Even though the name "Hoot" is on the dealership signs, I know full well that my family – that is my blood relatives and my work "family" – contributed greatly to our success. In the same way, Itsy knows that his wife, son and daughter, have been his support throughout his life.

Like me, Itsy is still working and active at an age when most people are slowing down. Thank goodness for that, because he's committed to sharing his joy and his wisdom with others. He has mentored countless people, he's given generously to many charities and has helped with many fundraising efforts throughout the years.

I've long thought Itsy should share his experience and wisdom with others. I'm glad to see he finally has, through the pages of this book. When I read it, I could hear Itsy's unique voice, telling the funny, heart-warming stories in his own way. Like Itsy, the book is always positive and entertaining, never mean-spirited, never scandalous.

Throughout the book, Itsy peppers his stories with life lessons to apply to your own life. Such lessons are always easier to take with a bit of humor – and there's plenty of that in "60 Years Young with Itsy".

I hope you enjoy "60 Years Young with Itsy" as much as I have. I've enjoyed reading it as much as I have enjoyed knowing him.

Hoot McInerney

Martin "Hoot" McInerney owns seven dealerships in Michigan. He was among the first auto dealers to create a nationwide dealership group. He is widely known for his business acumen and his generosity, having raised and donated millions of dollars to charity. He is a recipient of the National Football Foundations' Distinguished American Award and has many times been named Automotive Man of the Year and Automotive Executive of the Year.

INTRODUCTION

I'm Itsy Lieberman, "The Face of the Seniors," and I wrote this book because I can make a difference – especially for baby boomers and seniors! As a 60+ Baby Boomer, I am a walking success story and I want to share that success with everyone. I understand America – its greatness and its challenges.

There is a growing need and hunger for physical and emotional well-being in this country. There is absolutely no reason seniors and Baby Boomers can't participate and embrace these key elements of their existence.

How do I know this? Because I've lived it.

About me

I live in Troy, Michigan. In high school and college, I loved football, baseball, basketball and track. Later, I coached football and baseball (14 of my players signed professional contracts). I left coaching for a successful marketing career and worked with some of the biggest names in corporate America.

After a series of physical setbacks, I made up my mind that I was going to really live my life. I developed and practiced a program called Sunrise Chi, which I have taught for 38 years to people of all ages. I have a great passion and joy for teaching these exercises, especially to seniors, and for helping them to be calm and peaceful in today's chaotic world.

Itsy and Vivian

I am fulfilling my life's dream of helping and giving back. At the time of this writing, I teach Sunrise Chi at the Fleischman Jewish Assisted Living facility and at The Friendship Circle (a facility for those with autism). I am a proud board member of the Michigan

Jewish Sports Hall of Fame Foundation and am humbly honored to have been nominated for induction there.

So many people have improved their lives with Sunrise Chi that I believe I can help you, too. The rest of this book reveals the lessons I've learned in the locker room, in the board room, in the workout room, and in the family room. While they weren't the easiest lessons to learn, I've sure had a lot of laughs while learning them. Come laugh and learn with me.

For more information, visit www.60yearsyoungwithitsy.com or contact Al Horton at 248-535-0997 or at ahorton23@yahoo.com.

What's an Itsy?

When most people meet me, I can tell they wonder about my nickname – Itsy. Where did it come from? What's the story behind it? What's an Itsy?

I honestly don't know.

I've had that nickname for as long as I can remember. It could be because, at 5 foot 6 inches, I'm not nearly as tall as my basketball player friends.

It could also be from that song, "Itsy Bitsy Spider."

I've had the name since I was a kid but the song, "Itsy Bitsy Teeny Weeny Yellow Polka Dot Bikini," sure helped. It was a hit on the radio in my college days.

All I know is I like it. It suits me and it makes people smile.

CHAPTER
O · N · E

THE LOCKER ROOM

"It's not your age, it's how you age."

▶ ERWIN "ITSY" LIEBERMAN

Discipline is the biggest thing

The main thing I learned in the locker room was discipline. Believe me, I needed it. My background was "colorful," to say the least:

I was born on September 26, 1943, to Sam and Ida Lieberman. I was an only child. I was raised in Detroit, Michigan, on Grand Avenue. We lived in a three-flat house.

My Dad: A Damon Runyon Character

My dad came from the infamous "South Side" of Chicago, so he had plenty of street smarts. His personality was contagious. Everybody liked him. His personality was his calling card. That's probably why he became a good restaurateur. My dad had a big belly, always smoked a cigar.

Dad told me stories about being in the gangs. When they had gang fights in the playground, my dad was in charge of having the pool ball in the sock.

Dad came to Michigan in 1938 and met my mother, who was born in Detroit. They got married in the early 1940s. She was a sweetheart. My dad was always the face of the family, with his personality and charm. My mother always stood by him, saying, "Yes Sam." "Yes Sam." "Yes Sam." She was the perfect fit for him because he was always in the limelight. My mother was always on the sidelines, always very subdued.

Sam Lieberman and Jay

After my dad came from Chicago, he was a waiter at one of the mineral bathhouses in Mount Clemens. Back then, people would come from all over to soak in these bathhouses, even movie stars and

CHAPTER 1

athletes. People said the mineral baths were great for the skin and for overall health.

Dad also did other things I don't want to get into.

Once he made a little money, he was a partner in the Blaine Restaurant on 12th Street in Detroit, a very tough area. (Later 12th Street would be the place the Detroit riots broke out in 1967.) It was the territory of the Purple Gang, the Jewish gang that ran that area. They were notorious for bootlegging, gambling, you name it. Dad had ties with them. He was colorful, charismatic. Everybody liked him. He had the restaurant for seven or eight years.

As time went by, my parents sold the restaurant. He looked around for another one and found the Avalon Restaurant on Linwood and Davison, another tough area. He had that restaurant for eight to 10 years.

An unusual bedroom

The Avalon Theatre, a movie house, was next door to the restaurant. It was known for its huge organ that someone would play between shows. Mom and Dad had to run the restaurant and, as I was an only child, they had to figure out something with me in the late night hours. So about 7 or 8 p.m. every night, they would take me into the Avalon Theatre to sleep. You could say the Avalon was my bedroom.

Bill Davidson, who became the owner of the Detroit Pistons, owned the Avalon Theatre. I came to think of him as a second father to me, because every night he had to come to the back of the theater and say, "Time to get up, Itsy."

My friendship with Bill lasted my whole life. When I was at (former Pistons Coach) Chuck Daly's 75th birthday party, I sat with Bill. So I asked him, "Who do you know the most out of all these people in this room?" He looked at me and said, "You, Itsy."

After about 10 years, there was a fire and that was the end of the Avalon Restaurant. My dad had to look around to find another place to run.

Dad was still looking around at other things, too, always looking for a piece of the action. He was a character's character and liked to gamble. He would bet on the horses and he would bet on the pinochle games. He liked to go to Sidney Hill, where all the guys would go for big card games.

Well, as you might expect, we went bankrupt – for the first time. Dad was broke. So in comes the guy I most respect: Morrie Fenkell. He was my first cousin. At the time, he owned a packing plant. Later he owned Liberty State Bank, which became Huntington Bank.

Morrie came in and supported us. He gave us money and he was responsible for my dad opening Sammy's Restaurant in Oak Park. Dad had that restaurant for 10 years – my bar mitzvah was there.

I want to mention here that I loved my folks, especially my Dad. And I respected him. I knew that he had to work hard and was trying to support us. It cost him a lot, in time, money, and stress.

While my parents were going through all that, I was a typical kid (except for my bedroom). I went to MacCulloch School on Windemere off Glendale in Detroit. (It's now known as Stewart Elementary and Middle School.) I took part in sports. Mom ran the home and Dad did what he could to keep us afloat. We were a pretty typical family for that area.

I must say that in all the time I was in sports, all the time I played football in high school and college and the pro leagues and with the kids, my Dad came to only one game. He was there for three innings before he walked away. But I never ever said, "Dad, you never came to my games." I appreciated him being my dad and making a living.

The start of my discipline

Still, I was growing up. One day, when I was in eighth grade, my mom and dad said, "You're going to have to go to a military academy. We're working every night until 2 in the morning. You have to go somewhere."

So I went to Roosevelt Military Academy in Aledo, Illinois, which Bill Davidson had recommended. At first, I didn't like it. That first year was scary and I felt I had been scorned, having to leave all my friends back home. At the end of the first year, I really didn't want to go back, but my parents said I had to. What else were they going to do with me, really?

After that, it was easier, though I never really liked it. (Who could like military school?) I worked up the ladder. I played football – halfback and safety. I played basketball even though I was only 5 foot 6. Between my junior and senior years, Roosevelt sent me to Ray Meyer's basketball school in Three Lakes, Wisconsin. It was a great opportunity for me, Ray Meyer being one of the greatest basketball coaches in the history of the game. He's even in the Naismith Memorial Hall of Fame.

I was at Ray Meyer's camp for four weeks and I liked it there. Ray Meyer liked it that I was Jewish because he had another player, Howie Carl, who was also Jewish and who was 5 foot 8, not much taller than I was and still on the short side for a basketball player. He taught us to dribble below the knees so the taller guys couldn't get it away from us.

Ray taught us well: Howie played for DePaul and was picked up by the Green Bay Packers in the '61 NBA Draft.

I didn't do so badly, either: When I graduated from Roosevelt, I won the most valuable athlete award. I was valedictorian. I was commander of the cadets. I met a lot of nice people in Aledo. I was offered some scholarships from Western Illinois and Carlton College, but I missed being home.

Crazy college times

I ended up at Eastern Michigan University in Ypsilanti. I
played football there for one year and I belonged to the Arm of
Honor, which is still known as the "crazy frat" at EMU. It's
where all the athletes went. Boy! Have I got stories from there.
In that one year we had five house mothers.

Put a fork in it

Here's one: One day, "Ma" put our lunch on the kitchen table.
They were hamburgers and we all grabbed for them. Soon
there was one just hamburger left and two guys grabbed for it:
Chuck Skiba and Conrad McRoberts.

Chuck glares at Conrad, "I'm getting that burger."

Conrad glares back and says, "I'm getting it."

They keep at it until Conrad put his hand over that burger and
glared at Chuck. So Chuck grabbed a fork and rammed it into
Conrad's finger. Man! Blood spurted all over the place! So Ma
comes running in and when she saw what happened, she
fainted! They had to take her to the hospital – all that over a
hamburger!

A little monkey business

Here's another one: My next-door neighbor was Norm Parker,
who was eventually named one of the top five defensive
coaches in history. Norm had this dog, Dugan, who would
always come down and run around, driving everyone nuts.

One of the other guys, John Lane, kept saying, "I hate that dog
-- he poops in my room. If Norm doesn't watch it, I'm going
to kill him."

So one day, John goes to the animal shelter and got a monkey
and brought it back to the house to kill Dugan. Poor Dugan

took one look at the monkey and took off running. The poor dog probably had a nervous breakdown. They never did let the monkey into the house – Dugan was bad enough.

I was only at EMU for one year but I made some great friends there: Norm, Tom Prieur, Pat Dingeman, Chuck, Conrad, John. We had some great times. There's a reason it was known as the crazy frat. But the friendships lasted: A few years ago, Norm Parker was named one of the greatest defensive coaches in the state of Michigan. I presented the award to him at the All-State. I'm proud to say that I'm a friend of his.

Damon Runyon strikes again

The reason I left Eastern after that year was my dad went bankrupt again. As I said, he was a real Damon Runyon character – charming but often down on his luck. He even used my bar mitzvah money to try to get his own money back. Eventually, he got started again and owned the Raleigh House, a restaurant which did a lot of catering, including events for Ford Motor Company. Morrie Fenkell came to the rescue again and got nine guys to put money in to help us out. He was such a wonderful man.

I ended up enrolling at Wayne State University in 1964.

Once I got to Wayne State, I had to sit out the first year. But then I played football – quarterback and safety – for three years. We won the PAC championship one year. I had a great throwing arm so I played in shotgun formation because I was really good at passing.

That year, the Olympic Games were taking place in Tokyo. I watched the javelin and was hooked: It was unbelievable! The guy's running, takes two steps and throws this pole with a pointy thing on it for a phenomenal distance.

"Boy! That's for me!" I said. I had a tremendous throwing arm, a very strong, quick release, so I went on to throw javelin at

Wayne. I had a lot of fun playing at Wayne and I lettered in football and javelin. I liked the football team and I was liked by my teammates. I would hang out with Dempsey Harrison and some of the other guys down 12th street, really bad neighborhoods, and then I'd go out to Oak Park where we lived. I have a lot of stories from those days, too.

I get mad—and I get even

At one game, we were playing Western Reserve in Cleveland. I was out on the field in the shotgun and one guard missed his block and let his guy come. He hit me and broke my glasses. I had blood coming out of my cheeks so they called a time out. I ran to the locker room to clean off the blood and get another pair of glasses. Then we went into a huddle.

I was mad: I went up to the guy and said, "How does it feel, you son of a ---?" and I slapped him. Later in the game he missed another block and I got hit again. He hit me in the sciatic nerve and I went down and got knocked out of the game. You can believe I was mad. I had to do something.

I waited two weeks, till everyone forgot about it but me. Then I put Red Hot ointment on his jock strap. I put it in and then hurried out to the practice field before anyone saw me. Once I was out on the field, I kept watching for the fun to start. It didn't take long. All of a sudden, the guy starts yelling and screaming and the coach, Stan Marshall, looks at him and says, "What the...?"

You could say I was a practical joker.

As you can see, I like to have fun with people. I've inherited my dad's personality. We all got along, though.

Peter Larco's Birthday Party

Let go of your mistakes or they'll come back to bite you.

I remember this one game, Wayne against Allegheny, the year we won the PAC championship. I was in the shotgun as usual. The coach told me to make sure to lob the ball at this one guy, Hazelwood, on a post pattern. "Don't fire it like you always do," the coach said. "Just lob it. Let him run under it."

Well, in the heat of the moment, I fired it. I ended up hitting a lineman in the helmet. Allegheny intercepted it and we lost the game. It was the one game we lost that year.

When I came off the field, the coach was mad. He was livid, livid, livid. I knew I was in for it.

Hazelwood comes up to me and says, "Why did you do that?" I said, "Because I saw you broke open."

I hate losing close games because you end up reliving your mistakes. My mistake came back to bite me in this game in another way.

On Monday afternoons, we had "chalk talks". They'd show us the game films and talk about the game. That Monday, the coach showed the whole film and when he got to that play, he said. "Now, I want to show you our quarterback who likes to throw rifles rather than lob the ball, like he's told to do."

Then he let me have it:

"Itsy! Why did you do that when I told you to lob the ball?"

Before I could answer, Dempsey Harrison, our fullback, came up behind me in the dark and covered my mouth with his hands. I couldn't move them to speak up. The coach is yelling and yelling, "Itsy! Do you think it's funny?!" It's dark so he can't see what's going on.

Finally, the coach turns on the light but at that moment

Dempsey takes his hands away. So the coach has no idea what happened and really let me have it then. "Itsy! You're going down two notches!"

I knew I'd come back because I had a really good arm and he needed me, but he was really, really mad.

Where there's fire – there's smoke

Well, I was really mad too -- at Dempsey. So I waited. Again, about two weeks later, I was walking down the corridor with our manager to put on my gear. We were passing the coaches' office when I said, "I'd hate to be Harrison when they find out about the cigarettes in his locker." (I should know – I'd put them there.)

All the coaches heard it. I made sure of it. They came out and I told them that Harrison left his cigarettes in his locker. So the coaches all went down to the locker room. And Bob Hurley opened his locker. Sure enough, there were cigarettes in there. Dempsey walked into the practice room. I ran out on the field to make myself scarce. I snuck back in though. Dempsey was in shock, "But, I don't smoke! I don't smoke! Someone must have put them in the wrong locker! I don't smoke."

Coach made Dempsey walk 300 yards in a squat walk. (Try doing that sometime. It's a killer.) So now, Dempsey was livid.

Later on, I was walking home with Dempsey. I took him aside and I said, "I think I know who did it. I think DeAngelo put the cigarettes in your locker."

"He did?"

"Yeah, I saw him going into your locker."

"You did?"

"I'm gonna get him…"

(Sorry DeAngelo, I don't think Dempsey ever found out the truth. Until now.)

I told you I was a practical joker.

Softball has been very, very good to me

As for baseball, I had a chance in 1961 to pitch for Cincinnati's Class D team in Waterloo, Iowa. I said no because I didn't want to be so far from home and I wanted to go to college. I did manage to stay in sports, though.

I wound up playing professional slow-pitch softball for the All Pro League. There was a league of six teams, including Little Caesar's, Snyder's, Dino's and some others. I pitched and I was also second in the lineup. I was a pretty decent hitter. I played for about five years. You'd have to pay to see us play but we didn't get paid.

One time, we were playing against Little Caesar's, who were the world champions. Before a game, I was always very, very focused. I didn't talk to anyone. I wanted to get my karma.

Sam Young and Eddie Crass, my two best friends, said to me, "What's wrong with you?" I said, "I don't want to talk." "But you've got to be thinking of something." I said, "You'll see."

So I go out to the mound and the first batter was up. I threw the ball and ran at the hitter and then I zigzagged. Everybody said, "What's that?" and they threw the ball back to me. I kept doing it: I ran up to the mound, put my foot on the mound, threw the ball but instead of going back I ran in a zigzag, trying to drive the other team crazy and maybe even get them to hit me. Little Caesar's was the world champion that year and I needed every bit of ammo to even the odds.

Little Caesar's had this catcher named Tex Collins, who was a real moose: 320 lbs. He could hit a slow-pitch out of Tiger Stadium. When I came up to bat a second time, he called me every name in the book. I just looked at him and said, "Tex, you couldn't hold my jockstrap."

That really got him mad. When he came up to bat, I threw the ball and he dribbled down the first base line. So I picked up the ball and ran right along with him. Roy Lombardo, the Little Caesar's manager, went nuts. He said, "I don't think they can do that." But the umpire said, "There's nothing in the rule books that said he can't."

At the end of the game, Little Caesar's did beat us but only by 7-6 when usually they'd hit 20 homeruns a game.

Whether it was slow-pitch, football, or javelin, I really enjoyed my playing days. When those days were over, I wanted to give back. These days, I'm on the board of the all-state teams and I give out the All State Division 3 Scholar Athlete Award every year. I'm proud of that.

My first coaching job

When I graduated in 1967, Tom Prieur said, "Its, I'd like you to come out to Lake Orion to coach our football team." Lake Orion is one of Detroit's northernmost suburbs. It's a beautiful area, all lakes and rolling hills. Lake Orion High School is a great school but the football team needed some serious help: They'd lost 20 games straight.

Tom and I worked out an arrangement. We decided I'd take the junior varsity team and be the assistant varsity coach. We had to find something to break the losing chain and start to win. We knew they couldn't have a winning season that year. So the idea was we'd work with the kids coming up in JV. As they improved and moved up into varsity, the varsity team would automatically improve. It worked: That first year, we brought the JV record to 6-3.

'What goes around, comes around'

I'll never forget we played Troy High School. Their JV coach just killed us. The score ended up 48-14. They really poured it on.

After the game, I told the coach, "Let me tell you something, pal: What goes around comes around." And I walked off the field. When we played the next year, we beat them and ended up 8-1. That really started the Lake Orion trend. They're still a power-house to this day. (He came after my time but Zak Keasey, a former student, later played professional football for the Washington Redskins, San Francisco 49ers, and the New Orleans Saints.)

I really enjoyed it at Lake Orion but then around 1970 Tom Prieur went to Florida and Larry Masteller said, "I'd like you to come to Detroit Country Day. You're the guy I need."

Larry was the football coach at Detroit Country Day, an elite private school. If you were among Detroit's rich and powerful and you had kids, you sent them to Detroit Country Day. It was well known in the area, particularly for its athletics program.

Larry and I were co-coaches. I was on offense. That first year, we were ranked at about 500. The next year, we were eighth in the state. There were a lot of good people: We had Mike Page. We had Larry Zangas. We had Robin Williams, Microsoft CEO Steve Ballmer, Mike Ilitch's kids and a lot more really good people. I was also assistant basketball coach for John Hannett. I was baseball coach too. We did really well and I enjoyed it.

Leaving at the top of my game

But when you're on top, sometimes that's when it's time to go.

Because our team moved up so far and so fast, a lot of people took notice. I was offered a chance to be backfield coach for a college club team at Eastern and at some other schools. I told the folks at EMU I would take it, but fate intervened.

One day, a man came to me and said, "I like your persona. I think you're a gentleman and you're really nice to people. I've been watching you. I just split with my partner and I'd like you to be my sales manager."

Me? In marketing? I said, "No. I'm too engaged in my athletics. I love the kids. I love to mentor people as a coach."

The guy asked, "How much can you make as an assistant coach?"

I said, "About $18,000."

He said, "I'll give you about $50,000."

That was big money for the 1970s, so I told Country Day I was going to take a leave of absence for a year. They said okay – and I never went back. I'll tell you more about that in the next chapter.

Once a coach, always a coach

When I left Country Day, I thought I was done with coaching too. And I was, for about 12 years. I went back when my son Jay was in Little League and in travel teams, including a Mickey Mantle 14-and-under travel league in Farmington. Jay wanted me to coach so I took the team.

I had 80 kids try out for it. We had three people doing the judging at tryouts, so it would be fair. Well, I ended up having to cut my son. I didn't want to do it, but I had to go with the best players. He was very good about it. He said, "I understand Dad. I understand." I made him a sort of assistant coach because he didn't have the wherewithal to be a starter. He was a really good assistant too. I'm not saying that just because he's my son, either.

We went 24-0: we didn't lose one game. Mike Modano, who went on to play for the Red Wings and the Minnesota North Stars, was second baseman for Westland, and we beat them. We finally got beat in the regionals.

For the boys

They wanted me to take the 15 and 16 year old team the next year. But I wanted to take a summer off -- we had bought a cottage in Charlevoix and I wanted to enjoy it.

That plan didn't work out. The kids who were in my 24-0 team were now in the 15-16 level and they won hardly any games at all. They didn't have a good record those two years. So the parents came to me and said, "You've got to come back. They're going to be juniors and seniors and there's scholarship money on the line."

I didn't want to do it, but it was for the community and for these kids so I took it back for two years. We went 58-4. I had some great players.

The Secret to My Success

If I were writing a book (which I have) and I wanted to say how I did it, I'd say this:

The first thing I always do is have a meeting with all the parents. I tell them, "I'm happy to coach your kids. It's an honor for me to do it. However, I am the coach. If any parent does not agree with what I'm doing, you and your son will leave. Or, if another parent says to another kid's parent, 'This kid shouldn't be playing,' or 'You should be playing,' you'll be outta here."

I also tell them, "I run this team. I'm not getting paid for this. I'm doing it because it's for the community and I'm doing it because I love the kids. So I ask you as a gentleman: Don't get in my way when I'm coaching your kids."

Play for your team, not for yourself

I always coached for the kids. It wasn't about the money for me. I wanted to get the kids to play as a team. Some parents would push back a little about that. They kept pushing me to have their kid start.

I remember one mom came up to me, "Is he going to pitch today?"

"No."

Then, the next day, "Is he going to pitch today"

"Yes."

Then the next day, "Who's going to pitch today?"

I looked at her and said, "You are."

She got the drift. I meant, "Don't bother me."

It's not about the money, but it is

I can really appreciate that parents want their kids to be the best player. However, it's very hard for a coach—he has the responsibility to his team and to his coaches and to his players and to their parents. But I always tried to be fair to people. If a person didn't start, I always tried to keep them up. You see, if he gets down on himself, it's infectious and it affects the whole team.

The money in sports is so big that a lot of people from poor homes want their kids to sign contracts for football and baseball. The same is true for singers. I think that all that glitz and glamour – and I mean all professional sports and entertainment – is all about the money. It's especially true today. Just recently I heard about a kid at Notre Dame, a full back. He and his dad got in a fight because he thought he was a better player than the coach thought he was. It happens all the time, but it shouldn't be like that.

Leadership counts

Like my friend Chuck Daly said, "You've got to have a leader that can run a team that they all look up to."

One of my players was Jeff Calcaterra, who was drafted by the New York Yankees. I said to him, "You're going to manage this team from a player's perspective. And if you can't go to a guy, 'you'd better get running' or whatever, then I'll take it under my jurisdiction and they'll be gone."

Those were my rules. We all abided by them. We all had fun and stuck together. I'm proud to say that 14 of my kids signed Major League contracts: three went into pro football. The one who made it the biggest was Jim Miller, who played for the Chicago Bears – he was my No. 2 pitcher. He was drafted into baseball in the 16th round and then he went on to football.

I was always very cordial to the parents. I would tell the kids, "Let's go out and play, but we play with class." For instance, I told them, "If you see a kid bobble the ball, don't laugh at him or razz him. Class wins."

Sure, I'd prefer to win. But I always tried to be encouraging. When we lost, I would to go up to the player and say, "It's over. Keep up your head up." The next day is the next day.

Character counts too

It's not all fun and games as a coach. There is a bit of unpleasantness too. One time, Detroit Country Day went to New Jersey to play a team there. The soccer team went too because they had a game as well. On the bus trip there, I could smell something wasn't right.

"Someone's smoking on this bus," I told Larry Marsteller and Barkley Palmer, the soccer coach. Smoking was definitely against the rules.

They didn't believe me and I couldn't find the source of the fumes, so I waited – and watched. After the game, on the trip back, I smelled the smoke again.

At a rest stop, while the guys were inside a restaurant, we coaches searched the bus and found the cigarettes. It was in a seat occupied by, among others, Mike Schlegel, the son of the headmaster.

"Tell you what," I told the other coaches, "Take six of them out of the pack and put the rest back." Nothing more was said the rest of the trip.

But as soon as we got back to the school, I pointed out the three guys who had been sitting in the seats where the cigarettes had been found. One by one, I called them into the office.

"Were you smoking on the bus?" I asked them.

"No coach, I wasn't," they each said.

"Then what's this?" I said, holding up one of the cigarettes.

Caught red-handed like that, there wasn't much they could say. I was furious. I talked to all the coaches about it.

"What do you think?" I asked them.

"We've got to follow the rules," they all said.

At that time, being caught with tobacco products meant an automatic expulsion from Detroit Country Day. I had to go to Dick Schlegel and tell him.

"Okay then, I'll do it," I said.

When I got to his house, he already knew.

"What are you going to do?" I asked him.

"Oh come on! Boys will be boys," he said.

"I see, boys will be boys," I countered. "You've always said that we can't bend the rules. If you don't stick to the rules this time, I will go to the board about this."

In the end, Schlegel expelled his own son from Detroit Country Day. It was a tough call, but the right one. You can't play favorites. Ever.

Make 'em Laugh

In addition to enforcing the rules, I did a lot of stuff behind the scenes to get my team an advantage. Before a ballgame, I'd go to the umpires and I'd tell them. "Listen, I'm playing for a championship. If we're winning and there's a bad call, or what I think is a bad call against my team, I'm not going to run out there and be crazy.

"But if it's a tight game or we're losing and my players are not playing up to standard and you call a ball that should have been a strike or whatever, I'm going to come out there and I'm going start ranting. But it's not going to be 'You son of a ---!' Or, 'what the h--- do you think you're doing?' While I'm kicking the sand and stomping around, it'll be things like, 'what did you have for breakfast?! I knew your grandfather!' I'll say all sorts of things but I won't say that you made a bad call."

When the umpires saw my antics, they'd start laughing so I had them on my side. I never saw an umpire or a referee ever reverse a call but I have a team to lead and if we're not playing well I've got to run out to spark them.

I was really happy with the kids we had. They were all great guys. I still keep in touch with some of them. I had Greg

Detroit's All-Time Greats
All the greatest athletes I've played with and known are humble. They don't talk about themselves, they talk about others. In my opinion the real greats in Detroit sports were:

Hockey: Gordie Howe and Ted Lindsay

Baseball: Willie Horton and Al Kaline.

Basketball: Chuck Daly, who led the Bad Boys, and Isaiah Thomas.

Football: Joe Schmidt was the all time best of the best. A lot of people would have said Barry Sanders but Schmidt has my vote. (I'll tell a story about him later on). The Lions now have Jim Schwartz, Kyle Vanden Bosch, and Matthew Stafford but the hero of the Lions is Joe Schmidt, who won three NFL championships as a player in the 1950s. He was All-Pro 10 years in a row and is one of the top five linebackers in the NFL. He's in the college and pro football halls of fame.

Hager, who went with the Tigers, Doug Fitzer who went with the Seattle Mariners. Marty Wolf went to the Brewers. Leo Hutchinson went to the Reds. Brian Dubois went to the Tigers. Calcaterra went to the Yankees.

Jason Wolf was a tremendous football and baseball player. He could have gone to the major leagues but he stuck with football. Now he has the all time record in the history of the Southwest Conference for receiving. He was with Dallas. Jimmy Miller went to the Bears and was drafted by Kansas City. Ricky Karcher went to the Atlanta Braves.

My favorite memory is when we went to a tournament for the top 24 teams in the nation. We ended up second – second in the entire nation. It was a great thing.

Scouts have to think of everything

As a coach I got an inside look at the college recruiting process. I had not realized until then how much was on the line and how many details recruiters have to pick out.

For example, I got a call from the New York Mets. They said, "We're going to draft Ricky Karcher." He was 6 foot 6 and had a 90 mph ball. He was a great first baseman. He went to Indiana University.

Along with all the other questions they asked me, the Mets scout said, "We've got to ask you, how does he get along with Jennifer, his girlfriend."

"I thought you were drafting Ricky," I said. "What does Jennifer have to do with anything?"

"Do you know how many kids we lose? Do you know how many kids we have there who have girlfriends? The guys go down to the minors and there are all those girls from small towns who start hanging around," the scout says. "One day, his girlfriend calls him and he doesn't answer the phone. Then, the next day, he calls her and she doesn't answer the phone. So they get in a fight and he loses his concentration on baseball – the reason he's here in the first place. It always happens. So, how does he get along with Jennifer?"

I said, "I bet he'll marry her." And he did.

Jim Schwartz
In my opinion the Lions are very lucky that they now have a great coach in Jim Schwartz. I know Jim really well and I respect him. I had the honor of being asked by Coach Matt Kives to give a pep-talk to the sixth grade football team, which was undefeated and heading to the championships. Jim Schwartz' son is on that team and before my speech I told the boy I knew and respected his dad.

After my speech I had the team circle up and put their hands in the middle to chant, "We are relentless."

The following Monday, I met Jim at the Hard Rock Café with Kyle Vanden Bosch, Lions' Senior Vice President Bill Keenist, and Dan Miller, the Lions' play-by-play announcer where they were taping a radio show. Jim mentioned my pep talk and I expressed my admiration for the team and his son.

"I told them, 'We are relentless.' Don't you forget it too, Jim," I said. He laughed.

I predict that under Schwartz' and Vanden Bosch's leadership, the Lions will win a Super Bowl.

Ilitch Generosity

The Ilitches treat everyone well, in big ways and in small ones, too. They don't like to blow their own horn but I have to tell you about one very kind thing they did for me:

I remember once Mike Bayoff got me tickets to the Fox Theatre, which the Ilitches own. Mike is the Senior Director of Communications for the Red Wings, which the Ilitches also own. It was one of those nights in Downtown Detroit when everything was jumping. I couldn't find a place to park. I tried to get into the parking structure but was turned away.

Fortunately, Dave Agius, one of the chief officials at Caesars, was nearby at that moment. He told the gate guard in no uncertain terms, "That's Itsy Lieberman. Give him whatever he wants." I've always been grateful for that. It's just one small example of how the Ilitch family and their colleagues remember people.

Look at the coach – then at the athlete

I was very close friends with Bob Morgan, the coach at Indiana. Now, I love Michigan. I love Michigan State. I'm very proud of my state. However Bob Morgan took a liking to my kids and maybe the way I coached. He came to some of my games and he wanted my kids. At Indiana they call him a drill sergeant, though. He won't let you lose. I sent him a lot of guys. They all got full- ride contracts because of their attitude, which they developed from the way I coached.

Morgan said he always look at the coaches more than he does the kids. He'd say, "I know the coach I want. I want one who gets the discipline out of the kid and gets him to work as part of a team. If the kid is a prima donna, I don't want him. I'll cut him the first week."

Bob liked me so much he invited me to speak to 400 coaches at the Indiana Baseball Coaches Convention because of my record. He was a tough guy, maybe from having been a drill sergeant in the marines, but we got along really well. I even met Bobby Knight, "The General" himself.

Anyway, at the convention, I told the story about what I told the umpires, complete with getting in the umps' face and kicking the dirt. They loved it! All those guys called Bob and said, "That guy was the funniest I've ever seen. I learned so much by laughing at his stories. You've got to get him back."

I'm so proud that I coached. I've met so many good, nice people, including the kids, their parents, the officials and the coaches I was at the right place at the right time.

Lessons from the Locker Room:

Discipline is the biggest thing

Work ethic makes a great athlete.

Play for your team, not for yourself.

If you make a mistake, let it go or it will come back to bite you.

If you're going to be a coach, you've got to be a leader. If you're going to be a leader, you need a reward. In coaching, the only reward is winning.

It's not how many home runs or how many tackles, it's how you are off the field. When athletes shake people's hands, say "please" and "thanks" and treat people with dignity, those are the athletes I respect. A lot of the big athletes get in trouble for drunk driving and other things, but you won't find one negative thing on Joe Schmidt, Al Kaline, Chuck Daly or Ted Lindsay in the paper. Those are complete professionals.

Speaking of sports, I have to give special kudos to the Ilitch family. I'm great friends with Mike and his wife, Marian. I've known them since the late '60s. I taught their kids at Country Day. I've been in some business deals with his nephew, Mike Bayoff. If his kids—Christopher, Ron, Mike Junior, Lisa, Denise, Atanas, or Carole—ever need any advice, I will gladly give any help I can.

The Ilitches deserve more credit than they have received for doing so much for the youth of Detroit. They don't take credit because they are so unassuming. If it wasn't for the Ilitches, the city would not be in as good shape as it is.

CHAPTER
T·W·O

THE BOARD ROOM

"It's not about the money, it's about the money."

▶ ERWIN "ITSY" LIEBERMAN

I always told myself when you're on top, get out and go somewhere else because when you're on top, you're a hero. The next year, when you lose, you're a bum. I was eighth in the state at Country Day, so it was time to move on.

As I said in the chapter one, I had some offers to go in as a backfield coach at a couple of colleges, including EMU, my alma mater. I had told Eastern's head coach that I would do it, when, out of nowhere, this guy comes up to me who knew my dad.

He said, "I've been watching you. I know your dad and you would be perfect for me. I split with my partner and I'm reorganizing. I have a little store on Seven Mile and Schaefer. I would like you to consider coming with me as a sales manager."

I said, "I don't know anything about sales. The only thing I know is a football goes under your arm and that you look at the catcher for a sign. That's all I know."

The guy looked at me and said, "You're a winner. You're charismatic and I like the way you handle yourself. I think you'd be as good as a sales manager as you are as a coach."

Marketing Award

So I went to Dick Schlegel, the headmaster at Country Day and I said, "Dick, I'm leaving. I'm taking a leave of absence for a year. I was offered a job at a different venue and I want to try it."

"You can't do that," he said. "We need you."

"Dick, I need myself," I said. "I have two kids and a wife. This guy is offering me a lot more money than you can. I just want to try it."

A whole new ballgame

So that's how I started my marketing career – thanks to an offer out of the blue from Joe Valenti. (That's a good Jewish name, isn't it?) Joe was 25 to 27 years older than me. So I figured that's why he wanted me to be the sales manager for his business, J.A. Valenti Associates. He was over 50 years old; he'd just split with his partner. Meanwhile, I was in my early 20s. If things worked out, maybe I could be his successor in a few years.

Trouble is, I didn't know the first thing about marketing. I didn't know the first thing about anything. Joe's company sold incentives and promotional items – things like t-shirts, jackets, calendars, magnets, coffee cups, and other items emblazoned with company names. They also sold prize items for employers to give to their top customers and employees – things like anniversary clocks, jewelry, and so on.

I told my dad about my new job, and he said, "I know a guy real well in marketing. His name is Tom Hughes and he's at Chevrolet. You'd better go meet him."

I said, "Okay Dad. Thanks."

So I on my very first day of work, after checking in at our little shop at Seven Mile and Schaefer, there was Little Itsy walking through the door of GM World Headquarters, which is as big as 19 playing fields. I was in a suit. (Until that day, the only time I'd ever worn a suit was at the all-state banquet.) I went up to the receptionist's desk and said, "Hi, Ma'am! I'm Itsy and I'm here to see Tom Hughes."

She said, "Okay. Have a seat."

I took a seat and looked around, watching the people go by, all in suits. I looked down at my feet and for once, I didn't see cleats. I looked at my shoulders and for once, I didn't see shoulder pads. I said, "What the hell am I doing here?"

I waited a half hour and the receptionist said, "He's in a meeting."

To kill some time, I walked up to the receptionist and said, "You know what? I like you."

She said, "Thanks."

I said, "I'm going to go get a cup of coffee. Do you want some coffee?"

She said, "No."

"Well I'm going to bring you some anyway," I said. "And I'm going to bring you a doughnut."

I brought her some coffee and a doughnut and we started talking. "God Almighty," I blurted out. "I don't know what I'm going to do."

"Just relax," she said. "Tell me about yourself. What brings you here?"

I told her the whole story. "I was in sports," I said. "I graduated from Wayne State."

In short order, we got to be friends. We talked for some 20 minutes.

Then finally, she said, "Tom Hughes is ready for you. Go on up to the third floor."

I walked into his office. "Mr. Hughes," I said. "My name is Erwin Lieberman. Everybody calls me Itsy. Don't call me Erwin. Call me Itsy. I'm pleased to meet you, sir. My dad told me to come and talk to you. I'm new in this arena."

We sat down and talked for about 45 minutes. We didn't talk about General Motors or promotions or incentives. We talked about my career in sports. As it turned out, he had played college football. I gradually relaxed and got to feeling that I now had a friend in the industry. I figured this was my chance, so I leveled with him.

"Tom, I'll be honest with you," I told him. "I don't know the first thing about what I'm going to be doing. I don't know anything about it. The only thing I know is this: I'd like you to be my mentor."

"Absolutely," he said.

"Wow!" I said.

"Here's my house number, my office number, anything you want," Tom said. "I like you."

The good luck didn't stop there. When I got back to the first floor, the receptionist told me, "Itsy, I know your competition and I'm going to tell you when your competition is here."

"Geez," I said, "I've got two mentors?"

She said, "You're a gentleman. You like to laugh. I like you. I'm going to help you."

And that was the start of my relationship with General Motors. It was also the beginning of my education in marketing and the auto industry.

I should explain how the auto industry works. While the auto makers study all sorts of demographics to figure out what cars sell the most and why, they also work to build up relationships with the dealers.

Donald Trump and Friends

Car dealerships are franchise operations, independent businesses committed to selling a particular brand of car. The auto makers do everything they can to motivate their dealers to sell more cars, offering all sorts of incentives. If a car company has a good relationship with their dealers, they can guide the dealer to push particular models or options. On the other hand, the dealers can let the car companies know what customers are saying.

That's where I came in – my job (or rather, my employer's job) was to provide incentives to the dealers.

Friends in all the right places

The next week, I got a call from Tom Hughes. "I'd like you to come down to the GM Building," he said. "I've got something I want you to do for me."

I answered, "An order? Or is it to get you tickets to the ballgame?" (He knew I knew all the players.)

"No, I've got an order for you," Tom chuckled. "This is going to be your first one."

So I go to Joe Valenti and said, "You picked the right guy, Joe!"

I went down to the GM Building and Tom gave me an order for about $8,000, not bad for someone who didn't have a clue about marketing only a week ago. So I go up to Tom and he gives me the order.

"Oh my God, I've got an order!" I said to myself. It was like I could hear a marching band playing in my head. Look at me! I'm a professional marketer now.

Tom was the assistant marketing manager, so he took me to meet the big shots at GM. Then he took me to lunch. We had a great time, talking about such things as, "Is Colorado going to beat Michigan?" and so forth. All sports. As they say, it was the start of a beautiful friendship.

I was glad to have a friend in Tom Hughes and in his receptionist. Every time I went to see Tom, I'd greet the receptionist with, "Hey Baby Doll!" and she'd come around the counter and give me a hug. More importantly, she'd clue me in about what was going on at headquarters and help me to figure out who to talk to and when and how.

I'd call Tom sometimes at night and say, "Hey Buddy. Did you see the game last night? Goddamn! What a play!"

I told myself, "This guy, he's my buddy. I'm going to ride his horse. He is my racehorse and I'm ridin' him to the finish."

I picked a winning horse: I kept getting orders and orders and orders. I told Joe, "I'm not bringing you a lot of business, but I'm getting a lot of orders. I'm getting $1,000 here and maybe $6,000 there."

Beginner's luck

That all changed within a few months. One day, Tom called me. "Its, meet me at the St. Regis restaurant. I've got to tell you something."

At lunch he told me. "We're doing the presentation for the Chevy Honor Club, the biggest dealers we have. We give a gift to 5000 dealers if they hit their bogie, meaning their objective. We give them a $500 gift."

I did some quick math in my head. "That's $2.5 million."

"Itsy, your name is on the list of vendors in the running to provide the gifts," Tom said. "I put J.A. Valenti Associates Inc. on the list to purchasing myself."

I said again, "That's $2.5 million."

Tom said, "Sometimes you catch a pass and you run for 100 yards."

And what a pass this one was. Right then, I got the inkling that he was going to help me get that order. I felt it. And I wanted it more than anything in the world.

So I ran back to Joe Valenti and said, "Joe, we're in the running for the biggest award that GM gives – 5000 dealers at $500 each. What can we do? Let's do Lenox china. Let's do Waterford crystal. We've got to be solid, Joe. Come on! I don't know a lot about this. But you do."

So we worked and worked and worked, searching out products and negotiating for the best prices. It took a lot of time and effort.

Finally, the time came for Chevy to make the selection. Each vendor was assigned a space in a conference room with the three items it was offering to provide. Company X had a scarf, a coffee mug, and a clock. Our little company, J.A. Valenti and Associates, was in there with all the big guys. Among the items we had was a beautiful Waterford crystal vase. We worked our tails off to get a good price for it.

GM's big marketing people walked through the display to pick out what they'd order. Remember $2.5 million was a hell of a lot of money in the 1970s, so this was a big deal.

As I stood there, looking at all the other vendors and their displays, I got discouraged. "I've been doing this for four months. We're not going to get this. We can't get this."

Then I stopped myself. This was not the way to win the game. "No! I will win. Nobody's going to beat me!"

So I called my wife and told her, "I'm not going to be coming home until at least 8 o'clock every night this week. I'm going to get this order."

And I did. It took a lot of work and a lot of talking, but I got that order. They really liked the vase. They wanted something really high-end for their top dealers and nothing beats Waterford crystal.

I went to Joe and said, "I got the order! $2.5 million. We made good money on it."

I went to Tom and said, "Thanks Tom."

"I didn't do anything. You had the best thing."

"I had the best thing? I don't know the first thing about it. Thanks, Tom."

Tom smirked.

So now I knew I was in corporate America. That first year, I sold about $4 million. At the end of the year, Joe said to me, "I know I picked the right person. I knew you had this. People don't make $4 million the first year. Nobody does that. Nobody."

He gave me a check. I made $40,000 that year, really good money in 1971, especially for someone new to marketing.

Joe Valenti wasn't a dummy. Somehow he knew when I got $4 million worth of business that I would be a shining star to take over his business. Now he could relax because he got a guy he could trust, who also had a mentor in Tom Hughes. No, Joe wasn't a dummy. (I'm not either – most of the time.)

Joe Valenti gave me 30 percent of the company and I didn't have to pay one penny. So I got $40,000 and 30 percent of the company the first year free, one year after I left the football field.

I asked Joe, "Why did you do it?" But I knew why. I had been through this before. In football, if you have a winning season, they'll give you a raise because they don't want to lose you to the competition. I told him, "You did it because you felt I had certain qualities and I guess I did. I can't thank you enough for that. I'm having a great time with this."

I had become a part owner. After one year.

What do you do for an encore?

The second year, I accelerated like you couldn't believe. I got to know John DeLorean. I got to know all the big people at Chevrolet. They took me to the parts department. I was always on the bid list. I was just kicking ass and taking phone numbers. My second year I went up to $7 million. Imagine, the kid who slept in the back of the Avalon Theatre was now pulling in $7 million.

Then Joe called me into the office and said, "Its, I'm giving you 50 percent of the business for no money. You are my 50 percent partner. All because of what you showed me and the money we made in two years. We're 50/50."

I said, "Joe, thank you very much. I appreciate it. I don't know if I deserve it, but you must think that, you gave it to me."

Ever since Joe had given me that 30 percent of the company, I had been making plans for it. Now was the time to make one of them real.

I said, "Joe, I've been thinking. We're in this little place at 7 Mile and Schaefer and our office is so slow. You know, you did this for me and it's wonderful. But let's expand. We could really be a force with a bigger place in a more prominent location."

So we did. We got a Realtor and went all over, looking for just the right spot. We finally found a building in Royal Oak, Michigan, at 12 Mile and Main. The building used to be owned by Dondero Screen and Sash. Now we had storage space –

about 3,000 square feet and a nice entrance. After all, we were an incentives company. We needed to give our customers an incentive to come in and look around.

Academy Awards Memorabilia

I said, "We're in the big leagues now."

I knew a lot of athletes, so from then on the athletes would come to our shop. They were all great buddies of mine: Nick Eddy, the All-American from Notre Dame; Bill Munson, the quarterback; Frank Gallagher, the Lions guard; Steve Owens, the All-American. All those guys would come in and hang around. I liked them, and having them stop by was a great draw.

We developed a routine. All of us would go next door to Butler's Steak House for lunch. Every Monday, we'd meet at Bellanger House on 12 Mile and Main and talk about the last football or baseball game. We had so much fun.

They called this work?

Now, I'm really doing well at Chevrolet and I think things couldn't be better. Then, out of the blue I got a call from Pontiac Motor Division, saying, "We want you to come to Pontiac. We hear great things about you."

I asked Tom, "Did you tell them about me?"

He said, "I didn't do anything." And he winked.

Thanks to Tom, I now had the Chevy and Pontiac accounts. I'm excelling and a lot of people are getting a little bit jealous. I didn't let their comments get to me. I kept my head down and concentrated on my own work. Despite their jealousy, I was now feeling comfortable in my world. I really, really like it.

I hired this guy named Irv Reuben. He knew a lot about crystal and gold and was a real asset to the company. We were really, really doing well, so well that Joe and I were able to buy the building with cash, $120,000 cash. (We mortgaged it three times over the years so we could put in a showroom and other improvements.)

A new venture

Not only were we getting noticed at GM, our competitors were also taking notice. One day, an elderly gentleman named Al Padover came to us.

I knew who he was. My dad had told me, "You should buy out Al Padover, he has all the watches." (Meaning that Al's company provided those anniversary clocks and watches that people get on their retirement.) Al was a wonderful man, but at 82 years old, it was time for him to be thinking about retiring.

So I told him, "Al, let's be partners." He said okay and it was done: We were Padover, Valenti, Lieberman (PVL). We also hired Anne Hollingsworth, Al's right arm. She knew everything about watches and gold and everything. We couldn't have done it without her.

By now, we were making a lot of connections. For example, Former Michigan Governor George Romney came into my store every week. "Hey Its! How ya doing, buddy?!" He'd give me a hug. He was just one of the famous people who'd come in.

"Jesus Christ!" I'd say. "What's going on? How did I get here?" I became very passionate about what I was doing and it showed. I was very exuberant in all my dealings with clients. That enthusiasm drove sales. The company was exploding.

At this point, Irv Reuben went up to Pontiac to help me, since I still had Chevy as well. Then Buick Motor Division called and said they wanted me. Suddenly I had all of General Motors.

"How can this happen in six or seven years?" I kept asking myself. "I've got all this business. I don't deserve it. I just don't deserve it. I don't know what happened. But I'm not going to complain. We're doing well. Everybody gets along. We've got a showplace. This is unbelievable."

Irv and I got to do Buick's Sales Masters Contests. I was like a ringmaster in a three-ring circus: I'd go to Chevy. I'd go to Pontiac. I'd go to Buick. It didn't matter that they were competitors. It was all GM and all GM stock. If I'm making them money, it's all good.

I came up with all these crazy ideas, incentive contests. If you hit this bogie, you'd get this and so on. When a new product came out, I'd suggest ways to promote it to get people into the showroom. I was really, really enthralled with what we were doing.

Joe and I had Chrysler. I got to know the Executive Vice President Bob McCurry and Sales Manager George Booth. We had two of the Big Three, everybody but Ford.

"Who cares," I said. We were doing pretty well as it was. We didn't need to have the whole kit and caboodle.

That went on for a long, long time. We never had a bad year where we were in the red. Joe knew that I would someday take over the business, so I was learning all the time. One thing I learned was to take care of my people. I rewarded them, gave them bonuses.

"My son's birthday is Sunday," they'd say.

"That's great," I'd tell them. I knew a lot of ball players so I'd get tickets and give them away. "Take your son to a ballgame," I'd tell them.

I treated our people with kid gloves, as if they were royalty. I'd tell them, "I'll treat you as you want to be treated, human being to human being. I may be the boss here, but I respect you and I want you to respect me. Everybody's going to get along and we're going to make a lot of money. No confrontations. This is a family."

Joe had Wendy Blau doing all of his work. She was a very smart young lady, very creative. She was a big help to us. Meanwhile Irv and I were still going up to Buick.

We were a very versatile company: We had promotional products, we had incentives, and we had branding. It dawned on me that redistributing the work load could help Joe start to take things a little easier. After all, he was getting up in years.

"Joe, you can run inside," I said. "I can do outside."

So Joe was the inside man and I was the outside man, meaning he would handle people who came into our showroom while I visited the auto execs in their offices. I was bringing in $8 million to $10 million myself every year. From about 1971 to 1982 we had Jeep, General Motors. We were plenty busy.

Paul Hornung, Steve Lyons, Jack Nicklaus, Walter Douglass, & Itsy

But then Pontiac really started to expand. This guy at Pontiac -- Jim Graham, the executive vice president of marketing -- really took a liking to me,. He dressed to the hilt, a woman's man, a hot shot, a great guy, who really liked me. He also had a lot of power with the company – he could sign a check for $50 million if he wanted to.

"Its, you are my guy," he said. "I told purchasing, 'There's no bidding. Give it to Itsy.' I got my guy and that's it."

CHAPTER 2

Selling with the Stars

One of Pontiac's products was the KITT Car, from the TV Show, "Knight Rider" with David Hasselhoff.

Jim said, "Its, you've got Hasselhoff." He meant that I would be handling the marketing for all of Pontiac's tie-ins with the show, including its up-and-coming star.

"I do?"

"You got David," Jim said, expecting me to be impressed by handling a celebrity endorsement.

"But I don't know who he is," I said.

"You will. He'll know you better than you know him because I run this show," he said. "I picked the KITT car. We're going to California. I want you to meet David. I want you to meet his agent."

I went out there and met David Hasselhoff. When I met him, Jim said, "David, I want you to meet your new partner. You two are in this 50/50. We're going to sell all the KITT cars, clothing, and posters. Itsy runs that division. He's going with you to every auto show. He is your guy, got me, David?"

Of course David said yes. Knight Rider was his first hit show. From that point on, I was with Hasselhoff a lot. We did well. We had a good time. I liked him. He's a celebrity and celebrities can be cocky, but I knew how to handle him. We got along.

Much more important, from my perspective, was that the tours worked. Suddenly Pontiac was swamped with orders for Firebird Trans Ams that looked like KITT: black with a tan interior, a T-top and red scanner lights. We sold a lot of those red lights, too, along with the model cars and T-shirts.

We did that for four or five years or more. Whenever we had an introduction of a new vehicle, Jim Graham would give it to me to handle. Jim's buddy Howard Christie, one nice man, helped me at Pontiac also. He'd push for me. It was just one big happy family.

In every family, there's always some kidding back and forth. It was no different with our Pontiac family. We'd go out to California and Jim would say to me, "Pay the check."

I'd look at him and say, "You pay the check." He'd say, "Who's the guy that calls the shots and who's the guy that does the shots?"

"Both of us do," I'd retort. That's how we worked – together.

Jim took me everywhere. I was his go-to guy. We had glorious years during that regime – glorious.

Now we're in the '80s. We've got it all and still we're expanding. We did well and everybody who worked for us "did weller" as I'd say. We had parties to take them out to dinner. We gave bonuses of $20,000-$30,000 and the employees couldn't believe it. But that's the way I am and that's the way I'm going to be – I took care of my people.

Joe was getting a little older, about 75, and he had bad lungs. About 1986, I said, "Joe, want me to buy you out? I'll give you your money and you can go. You'll always be a part of this but you can go and starting taking it easy."

Joe said, "Its, I want to stay with my kids."

So I bought him out. I was 43 and had the company all to myself. Life was pretty good. I didn't think it could get any better than this.

'We ARE the Big Three'

Then all of a sudden, out of nowhere, comes a purchasing agent from Ford. His name was John Woods. "I want to talk to you," he said.

"About what?" I asked.

"Just something I want to talk to you about," he said.

I had no idea what he would want with me, but I couldn't help being curious.

"If you want to talk to me, I'd be interested," I told him.

"I want to talk to you in private," he said. "I'll make an appointment but it will be confidential."

We went to a restaurant and I said, "Yes, sir?"

He said, "I want you to take over the Ford business."

My jaw dropped. "What?!" I said.

"I want you to take over the Ford business," he said again. "I'm not happy with my suppliers. I went around and asked everyone. I asked them, 'Who's the best in marketing in the state of Michigan?' and everybody said, 'Itsy.' 'Itsy.' 'Itsy.'" So what do you think?"

"What do I think? We have Chrysler, We have General Motors. What do I think?! What are you offering me?"

"I'll give you a blanket order." He meant that Ford would have a long-term agreement with PVL. We'd get all the orders, no bidding against competitors.

I said, "Let me think about it. I'm going back to my team. I always tell my people what's going on. I want to get their input. They're the ones that deserve it. I'm just a figurehead."

I've always been a big believer in teamwork. If we all work together as a team -- everybody staying in his or her own lane and doing his or her own job -- it's always worked for me and it avoids the chaos that comes from animosity and jealousy.

So I called together my employees for a meeting to figure out how we could make this work. I said, "Okay, what do you think? I think we can do it but I'll have to give up Chrysler. Irv does a lot of it. I'll have to give up GM too. Luann, you're our receptionist. You're making about $25,000 plus bonuses. You're now taking the GM account."

Luann Shaw fell over. Imagine going from a receptionist's job to a GM vendor in the blink of an eye. But I knew if anyone could do it, Luann could. "I'm doubling your paycheck and that's what we'll do."

(She did fine, by the way, eventually taking on the Detroit Diesel account. It was thanks to her efforts that we did so well there. Oh sure, I was there in the suit and tie and greeting people, but Luann did all the real work.)

I knew I'd miss GM, but Jesus! We had to do it. Because we've got a blanket order and Ford's big. I was thrilled at the implications.

I told my staff, "Do you realize that now we've got everybody? We've got the Big Three. We ARE the Big Three. We'll probably be in the top 10 in the United States in branding. We've got to do it."

I went to Ford for my first order: 40,000 jackets for Ford Parts and Service. I got them done overseas. The money we made gave me all the money I needed to buy Joe Valenti out.

I said, "Joe, here's your money." I went around the room and gave everyone else money too, saying, "That's okay." "That's all right." I could afford to be generous and I wanted to be generous with these people who did so much. I couldn't help singing, "We're in the money."

I've always said, "I'm not a big shot." I'm just an easygoing guy you don't want to cross. We got the account and away we went. It was absolutely sensational, the way we worked together.

To tell the truth, a lot of Ford's management relied on me to ask who they should promote. They had confidence in me. I was around those people all the time. And because of that, they'd call me at home and say, "Its, who do you think we should promote to this level?" I'll give you four names. Give me your opinion."

I'd say, "I like Collins the best. I think he'd do a good job there." Then they'd say, "We've got a big opening. Somebody's leaving. Who do you think we should put in there, Its?" And I'd say, "Mondragon. I like him. Mondragon's good, put him in there."

Ford Family

I eventually got to know all the members of the Ford family – Elena, Bill Ford Jr., Buhl, Edsel, and Benson. The Fords were so great to me. I'm so proud and happy that I met them. They're a wonderful family. I have the utmost respect for Bill Ford, Jr., and the way he runs his football team. I also respected his dad and everything the family has done over the years.

When my dad ran the Raleigh House, his best friend was Henry Ford II. They used to smoke cigars together and talk. My dad catered most Ford events. Even though I started my marketing career at GM, by the 1990s I was very good friends with all of the Ford family.

The Fords always conducted themselves with class and dignity. Bill Ford was gracious enough to accept the Distinguished American Award from the Michigan All State Foundation when I invited him. He was so unpretentious. In the two hours that I was with him, I felt that I had known him all my life. We laughed and talked - - not about business, but about sports. He's the type of person I would love to have lunch with every week.

Edsel Ford, who ran the Lincoln Mercury Division, was always very classy, very informed. He always knew what he was talking about.

I really liked Elena Ford, when she was the head of marketing at Lincoln. I really liked her – we'd always give each other a hug when we met. She had a tremendous following because she was so bright. She attended an Ivy League school and has done a lot of good for the company.

Or they'd say: "Who do you think we should put here? Who's the toughest? We've got to have a tough guy to put in there at the top of worldwide direct market operations." I'd say, "Randy Ortiz. He's a monster. They won't mess with him."

Ortiz didn't know it. Mondragon didn't know that I helped him. Collins didn't know I helped him. All those guys didn't know I helped them. I didn't tell them. It wasn't about me. It was about getting the best person for the job.

Still more change

But as things come, things go. About four years later, I had to have bypass surgery. I had an exam for my insurance coverage and they found I had blocked arteries. At about the same time, Ford said, "We're going to go to one vendor for everything. You're our day-to-day vendor and you've got the call. But we're going to one vendor for all our branding."

A quick course in branding

An auto company spends millions of dollars developing, building and marketing a car before it ever sees the light of day. One slip-up means a loss of that huge investment.

One important key is the company's brand -- in this case Ford and Lincoln Mercury. The brand makes all the difference -- a marketer has to get that brand to the world in a timely fashion and with pizzazz.

Why does McDonald's sell more than Burger King or Wendy's or any other fast food place? Why does Geico get all that publicity? Why do people think of luxury when they hear the name "Lincoln?" If you market right and you know what you're doing, you'll win. But if you don't know what you're doing, you'll lose.

You have to know the demographics of who you're talking to and who is buying your car: Are you going after young adults, families with kids, or seniors? How are they going to use the vehicle: driving their kids to school and soccer? Going to client meetings? Just to run errands? That makes a brand.

If you don't understand those demographics, you're out of there. I've seen security guards go up to 50 people at a time and say, "You're fired. We're not happy with you. Pack up your things."

Branding and incentives produce a lot of ulcers. It requires a lot of aspirin because you're always hustling around and around. It can get to you. I found out that you've got a lot of politics, more than you'd think. Everyone wants to go to the top.

Linden Nelson's company had done a training project for Ford and was our main competition. Car companies use incentives to encourage distributors and service technicians to complete training programs so they'll be well qualified to service the cars. In addition to providing excellent service to their customers, publicizing the names of people who successfully treat those programs is great for building a car company's reputation for quality.

So here I am, about to go for a heart bypass and Ford is telling me, "We're going to one vendor for everything and it's going to be you or Linden Nelson."

In a circumstance like that, I knew only one company could survive. One company or the other would have to buy out the competition.

I said to Jim O'Connor, "I'm not buying him. He's going to buy me."

So I went to dinner at Morton's with Linden and our wives and we took a napkin and we wrote down the numbers.

Linden said, "I'll buy you, Its."

> **How the Auto Industry Works**
> The auto industry separates its workings into two divisions: product and non-product. Product means everything that goes into the vehicle – the steering wheel, the upholstery, the engine, etc. Naturally, that's the key part of the company. If something goes wrong with any component, it's a disaster. Generally, a car company uses the regular purchase order system in the product division.
>
> Non-product involves everything else, including "branding" the image that the car company wants for a particular vehicle. For instance, when most people think of "Lincoln Mercury" they think of a high-end luxury car. Non-product supplier relations are usually handled with a blanket purchase order to make it easier for a car company to have a unified branding effort.

I said "I'll take it. Except one thing: I still want 50% of the commission. That's a make-or-break condition."

Linden said, "But I'm giving you this much money and this much in salary." He pointed to the numbers on the napkin. They were pretty large. He was offering a lot of money.

I said, "Linden, I want 50 percent of what I bring in for my team and I want that in writing. You're buying my team and nobody knows Ford better than I do. I know everybody, every face at Ford and I've got to handle Ford myself. If you want to, you can go with me but I've got to handle them because I know them. I'm not taking over: You can be the chairman. I don't give a shit about being a chairman."

See, while a lot of people in marketing are out for power, I wasn't like that. I just wanted to make a good living for myself and my people.

"Then what do you want to be, vice chairman or president?" he asked.

"President," I said. "Let Bob Zocco (Linden's right hand man) be vice chairman. I'm going to run the Ford portion. I'm running it and I'm going to get 50 percent."

"God Almighty," he said. I drove a hard bargain – 50 percent commission is unheard of.

"Is it a deal or not?" I asked him.

"It is," he said. "Sign it."

That napkin was my contract. I wonder where the napkin went. That napkin made me the president of CCA (Creative Concepts in Advertising). PVL is gone. Here comes CCA with Linden as chairman, Bob Zocco as vice chairman and me as president. But nobody else was going to touch Ford or Lincoln. I had all the people.

Because of that napkin, I was getting a $200,000 salary, $1.5 million for buying the business and 50 percent of the commission. I knew I could make 10 times what Linden was making. I had put him to the test and I won.

> **Incentives**
> The auto industry uses incentives in many ways: Manufacturers offer incentives to consumers through cash-back incentives, loyalty programs, test drives, etc. Individual dealers also offer similar incentives to consumers. Manufacturers offer cash awards, travel, and merchandise. There are also incentives for parts sales.
>
> The auto industry uses advertising agencies for branding, including incentive programs. However, the agencies vary as to what services they provide. For example, most of the agencies I've worked for did not specialize in travel incentives. Other agencies specialized in training incentives etc.

We brought my staff over to the new business and it was an especially good staff. Best of all was my secretary Cindy Kelly. Linden, Bob, and I each had our own secretary and she was mine. She was a steadying influence. She was a real saint for doing what she did day in and day out. If it wasn't for her, we would not have gotten as far as we did. I really thank her for doing it all.

Anyway, we were doing really well. I got along well with Linden. (It helped that I was a black belt in karate: He didn't want to mess with me.) We became a good team: Linden, Bob Zocco, and I. Bob Zocco took over at GM. He's the GM guy; I'm the Ford guy. (We let Chrysler go by the wayside a little. We still had Chrysler but we didn't give it the attention the others had.)

Linden had a plane and I'll bet we put 50 million miles on that plane. Linden would listen to me because I was older than he was and I had a little status. We got along and everything was going along fine. We'd go to New York to bring in gadgets and clothing and silver and watches to offer as incentive products, which was going tremendously well. We were going along fine and I was happy.

Getting our Ha-Lo

All of a sudden, things changed. Lou Weisbach from a company called Ha-Lo Industries got in touch with us. Ha-Lo was on the NASDAQ, the only one in marketing and ad specialties of that type that was there. Lou wanted to get Ha-Lo on the New York Stock Exchange but he needed $100 million to do it. He called and talked to Linden and me and said, "We were going to buy you and we are going to make it worth your while."

Linden and I talked about it and we said, "We'll do it." We were doing $110 million in revenue and going with Ha-Lo would put us on the Exchange. We became Ha-Lo Creative Concepts.

Itsy goes to Wall Street

So Itsy goes to Wall Street along with Linden and my wife, Vivian. Lou Weisbach said, "It's great to have you, Itsy. I'm giving you a ton of money. I know you got the Ford account. You're a tremendous guy. By the way, do you know who's sitting with the chairman of Wall Street when they pull the opening bell the day we go on the exchange?"

I said, "Who?"

"You are!"

"I said, 'Shit, I don't know what to tell him. Get somebody else.'"

Lou said, "No. It's you. He'll like you. So you're sitting with him."

So I said, "Okay."

I ended up talking with the Wall Street chairman about football and other stuff. There was a big gathering. My wife was with us. It was a big moment.

Now Ha-Lo was on the New York Exchange. I am ecstatic. They gave me $50,000 in stock options. They gave me a great signing bonus and we're in the money and everything is going well. We're the number one company in the world in marketing and promotional products and incentives (except for travel, which our company didn't handle).

Ha-Lo's headquarters were in Chicago. Linden and I would go there every week to see how everything was going. And my team at Ford was doing really well. All of a sudden we started to explode on the Exchange. We went from $24 a share to $37 in a year or two. Unfortunately it wasn't to last.

All good things…

Then one day we were at a convention and we were playing gin up in a suite – me, Linden, Bob Zocco, and Marshall Katz, our CFO. Lou Weisbach calls us up and says, "I need to come up and talk to you for a minute."

It turned out that we "missed our number," as they say. We were at $37 but then our stock started to slip and we couldn't recover. We told ourselves, "It won't be that bad," but it was

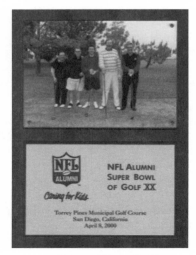

Torrey Pines Golf Tournament San Diego, CA - Celebrity Player Eddie Murray

bad. Our stock continued to tumble and we couldn't pull out of it. Suffice it to say that bad decisions had been made that affected our stock price. Stockholders noticed we weren't doing well and were asking themselves, "Just what does a marketing company do anyway?" That made them afraid to invest with us.

We went down and down for about nine years: from the '90s until 2001. We brought in a new guy, Marc Simon, as CEO to try to turn us around, but we ended up filing for bankruptcy under Chapter 11.

Linden was heartbroken. I was heartbroken. Everyone was heartbroken. I said, "Linden, we've got to do something."

Marc was doing his best to try to save what was left. One day he came to me and said, "Itsy, I'm going to ask you to do me the favor of your life."

"What do you want me to do?" I asked.

"Its, you're the top producer in the history of promotional products, set-ups and everything," he said. "Don't jump ship. I know you could jump ship easily because everyone is going to come after you. But please, don't do it. If you do, we will never get out of Chapter 11. They're all looking at you: What is Itsy going to do?"

I said, "What do you want me to do? I'm still selling Ford things. We're in receivership, but I'm still doing business at Ford. What do you want me to do?"

He said, "Please don't jump ship. Somebody will give you a ton of money to leave and Ford will take you. But I'm just asking you to stay."

I said, "Marc, you know what? I'm not going to jump ship. I'm staying and I'm going to do what I'm going to do. Whatever you want me to do, I'll do. But I won't jump ship."

So we stuck it out and we were able to stay with Ford. Marc said, "Itsy, you're a sensational guy for doing that. You helped those people, everybody'd be gone otherwise if you hadn't stayed. You saved this company."

I said, "So what?" All I did was what I thought was right. I couldn't protect my hide and let my team and their families lose their jobs.

Marc said, "I don't know how to say 'Thank you.' I'm going to make sure you get all your commissions, every single one." (Because when you're in receivership, the creditors will go after all your assets, including commissions, to pay their bills.)

I asked Linden, "What are you going to do?"

He said, "I just had a talk with Ford and I think I'm going to buy a company call Beanstalk. It's one of the biggest branding companies in the United States. It's something similar to what we're doing so Ford would want to buy it."

Ford? Ford is going to buy Beanstalk, a branding company for licensing? Beanstalk licenses celebrities like Mary Kate and Ashley Olsen. They do branding and incentives but they do it differently than in the auto industry.

"I think Ford is going to buy it and run it separately," Linden said. "They will be a partner."

I said, "Great! Good Luck."

He said, "Good luck? No. You're my luck. If they buy it, I told them I have to have Itsy with me."

So, they negotiated with me. I was going to be vice chairman of it in Detroit. They offered me a contract on a "best effort" basis, "best effort" meaning I didn't have any specific goals to meet, it was just assumed I was giving my best effort.

I said, "What! What are you talking about?"

An acquisitions guy comes to me and Linden stuck up for me and said, "I've got to have Itsy." I had helped Linden, advising him to go somewhere else if anything happens even as I told him I'd have to stay at Ha-Lo.

They offer me this contract. It's 20 pages long. I took it to my attorney, Harold Fried. Harold is my go-to guy when I get in trouble. I'm a person who, if I have a toothache, I don't go to a foot doctor. Nobody can beat Harold Fried.

"Harold, what are we going to do?" I asked him.

"Its, do it."

"What does the contract say?" I asked.

"It says you're going to get a ton of money," Harold said. "And it says you've got a best effort. That means you don't have to work. You've got a six-year non-compete clause and you have to stay for four years."

"I just have to sit there for four years? I can go to the casino? I can go to Red Run (my favorite golf course)?"

"You can go anywhere. You don't have to do anything. You sit there for four years. You're going to get a Jaguar to drive. They'll pay for all your health care and all the other stuff."

"I don't get it," I said. "I just don't get it."

Basically, the contract meant that Linden stayed on with Ha-Lo. (In 2000, Ha-Lo had entered a joint venture with Ford called iDentify to license Ford products as well as those of other companies. Now, Linden bought out the Ha-Lo portion of iDentify and Ford remained the majority owner. Several months later, iDentify bought out Beanstalk Group, and Linden became CEO and minority owner.)

Linden and I and the guy who does the acquisitions agreed to the deal. That led to one of the best things that ever happened in my life.

This new contract had to be signed by Ford President Jacques Nasser; Wolfgang Reitzle, the head lawyer for Ford; and two other people on the board. This was unheard of, especially for signing a vendor contract.

I said, "I'm not that important! How can the president of Ford be signing a contract for me?"

"Jacques Nasser, the president of Ford, and Wolfgang Reitzle have to sign it. We've never done anything like this before," they said. Their signatures were needed to show that this was approved at Ford's highest level.

Why did they do it?

One day, later on, I saw Jacques Nasser at the Townsend Hotel. I had to ask him, "Why did you did give me that much money to sign a best-effort contract?"

He paid me the biggest compliment I've ever had in my life: "Do you think we want you to go to Chrysler, to General Motors, to Toyota? To any other car company? We want you to sit there and have fun because we know where you are and that you're on our side. That's why we did it. You are that special to us."

I walked out and started to cry.

But I said, "I'm not going to just sit there. I'm going to help Ford and do what I usually do. I've got a big office. I've got a great secretary. I've got a board room. I've got everything. I'll just keep on doing what I do and see what happens."

That was the last big step of my career. I stayed there three and a half years. Then Ford said, "We're going to sell the incentive and promotional products company and we're going to go with another company." They had to buy me out and I was clear of corporate America.

Looking back on a career

I'm very proud that I was the top producer in the history of incentives and marketing and promotional products seven years in a row. (I turned it down in the eighth year because I said it's time someone else had a chance.) It was getting crazy and I didn't want to do it anymore. Over the years, I had gotten too many awards to count.

My blueprint for success

A lot of people have asked me how to be successful. So I'll tell you what I did – and what I didn't do.

When you get a big order – let's say it's a $1 million-deal – don't think that you're a big shot. Put the money in the bank. Don't buy a Rolls or a mansion or anything else – all you'll get is debt. When you have the money in hand, you'll feel secure and you don't have to worry. Then you decide what you want to do.

I've always lived an understated life. I don't brag about how much I have. I only want to know that my family and I are secure. A lot of people get overwhelmed with success and splurge on items they don't need, just to have those status symbols. Then when things turn around, which always happens, they're stuck.

I'll give you a scenario: Let's say you become successful. You have some extra money so you decide to buy a six-story building. Then, Coca-Cola or some other corporation comes along and leases four floors of your building.

"Great! I'm really making money now!" you say. So you buy a boat and a plane and all those other things you've dreamed of. After all, you're secure, right? You don't have to do anything at all. Just enjoy life.

Eight years pass. All of a sudden, Coca-Cola says, "We're moving. Someone else made us a better offer."

What just happened? You just went from security to being a liability. The bank still wants its money but you don't have anyone in your building. You'll have to sell it.

But, if you had lived beneath your means, you wouldn't have had to worry about anything.

In a nutshell, that's what happened to General Motors and Chrysler. They didn't watch their rears and it cost them. That's why they went bankrupt.

It's funny, but a lot of people are addicted to power. Suppose I gave you a choice: You can have a $100,000-a-year salary with a corner office and a staff of 50 people. Or, you can have a $200,000-a-year salary without all the prestige. Which would you choose? You'd be surprised at how many choose the first choice. Most people, in fact, want power. They don't care about the money.

Or, to put it another way, let's say again that you're really doing well. Your company has $5 million in the bank, thanks to your contract with the Big Three. But then, the car companies cancel your contract, cutting off 80 percent of your business.

What are you going to do?

You could take your $5 million, dissolve your business, give bonuses to your departing employees to thank them for their hard work and live on the rest (quite comfortably, I might add).

Or,

You could take the money and blow it at the casino. You keep telling yourself, "I'm on a roll. I'll make it all back."

That's what happened in 2007 and 2008 in corporate America. The big shots took big gambles – and lost.

I'm not like that. I'm not a big fan of hot shots, who let their egos get bigger than their brains. That's why I'm so happy at Red Run Golf Club. A lot of my friends there are very successful, but they don't talk about it. They don't care about it.

I say, "Just take care of your own self and your family. Don't worry about anyone else."

The fun part of marketing

I have to tell you some things about corporate America that were really fun.

I mentored Howie Long, the football player. Jack Gilardi, who's like a brother to me, was his agent. He asked me, "Who do you think we should get to launch the Expedition?" I said, "Howie Long."

We did and we gave him $75,000 to do it. Then we got Howie a $300,000 contract for two years to do "Built Ford Tough."

Handling marketing incentives was great fun. Here are some of the things I did.

I did the Shopping Spree at Neiman Marcus. I closed the Neiman Marcus store for three years on December 14 for 125 dealers who hit their objective. The dealers got the run of the most luxurious store in America to buy gifts for their families and friends – and maybe themselves, too.

I liked doing vehicle launches. I did the Expedition launch. I did the Navigator launch. But of all the launches I did in my career, the one I liked the best was the U.S. launch of the Ford Focus in 2000. Ford said, "This is one of the biggest launches we'll ever have in terms of demographics – from 18 to 30 year old people."

We had a committee: Jan Valenteck, Lon Bollembacker, Joe Castelli, Julie Rheaume, and me. We all knew we had to make this work. Ford was counting on this.

Focus-ing on "La Vida Loca'

We started the launch by taking Ricky Martin – we wanted to go to the Latinos and he was riding high with his single, "Living La Vida Loca." We sent him all over the United States on a tour of 24 cities in 1999. After his performance, we had about 20 models go outside the arena and when the kids would come out they would get to sit in the Focuses. We'd pass out all sorts of paraphernalia.

Marketing Award

Then we gave out G-shock watches to the first 50,000 people who bought a Focus. It was a new watch that was really hot at the time, especially among young adults.

'American Idol'

That tour went so well, the advertising firm J. Walter Thompson came to us and said they wanted us to sponsor "American Idol." We looked at it and it had Randy Jackson, Simon Cowell, Paula Abdul, and Ryan Seacrest. We talked about it and talked about it. They wanted $21 million for the sponsorship. Some people said, "There are no names, why would you do this?"

It was because of the demographics. American Idol was going after the exact same people Ford was going after with the Focus. We didn't need the big names – American Idol was going to be the big name. We could sense it.

It wasn't my first time working without a big name celebrity. When I was at Pontiac in the '80s, we launched the Firebird. Remember, David Hasselhoff was a no-name then and he had the KITT car. He was our partner. That launch put Pontiac at the top of the heap. That's why I felt we should do it with American Idol.

Besides, if we wanted to get someone who was a superstar, we'd have to pay him $50 million to launch something.

"Let's do it," we said.

So we did. The rest is history. I went to California. I talked to Randy Jackson and the rest of the cast. I sent them goodie bags every month. I put in all the Ford stuff -- pens, jackets, what have you. "Give them to everybody, cast, crew, everybody," I said. Ford has American Idol. Let's do it.

It was a really great experience and as everyone knows, the show was hot. At that time, I knew Pudge Rodriguez, the baseball player. We were very good friends and he said to me, "Itsy, Hoot told me you know people from 'American Idol'."

"Yes, I do."

"Well, my daughter's birthday is coming up; can you get four tickets for the last night of the show? It's right around her birthday. She'd love it."

"For you, Pudge, I'll do it," I said. So I got four tickets for the finale at the hottest show on TV. Everyone wanted those tickets, but Pudge got them. He went backstage and talked to all the people. His daughter was about 11 or 12 and she was thrilled. He never, ever, ever stopped thanking me for that.

Looking back, I'm amazed at how well I did. I sold $370 million worth of watches, T-shirts, everything you can imagine. That was my stint in corporate America. When they gave me my last check, I took it - $800,000 — and I walked out.

"I am through with corporate America. It never changes," I told myself. "It's all about politics. It's all about people and I had enough of it. I always said I would get out on top. I got out on top and I'm not going back. I'm out of jail!"

Don't get me wrong. I liked marketing. I met so many nice people. I went to 24 Super Bowls in a row. I met Ryan Seacrest. I've shaken hands with athletes, with movie stars, and with presidents. It was a great run.

Glitz, glamour – and stress

Marketing is glitz and glamour, just like the movie industry. You go to the best hotels, eat the best food. You go to the best golf courses. You go to every event. I liked it. Linden had his plane so sometimes we took his plane.

But there's an incredible amount of stress. There's always a deadline to meet. There's always somebody breathing down your neck trying to beat you. You're on the road all the time, missing all the stuff that goes on at home.

My biggest crisis

As an example, I'm going to tell you about the biggest crisis I ever had in marketing. I'm not going to name the person responsible. He'll know when he reads this.

Hoot McInerney (right)

At Ford, we had what was known as the 100 Club for the top 100 dealers, who were treated like royalty. I did all the things for the 100 Club's events – I got the rooms and everything. I was a master at it. We had Barry Manilow, Bill O'Reilly, and Chuck Daly come to their events. We had Billy Cunningham – one of the greatest basketball players of all time. He won a championship. He's the only guy who played on a championship team, then coached a championship team and then owned a championship team - the Miami Heat. I met them all. It was really great.

One year, the head of marketing said, "I want (a former U.S. president) to speak at the 100 Club."

They said to me, "Do you know anybody who knows him?"

I said, "Yes I do."

They said, "Who?"

I said, "Hoot McInerney." (Hoot is probably Detroit's most prominent car dealer. He's also quite a generous philanthropist, so he knows everybody who's anybody and they know him – and like him.)

They said, "He does? Well our executive vice president wants him to come to the 100 Club. Its, will you arrange it?"

"Yeah, I'll arrange it."

Hoot called the president, "Would you come to the 100 Club? We're going to pay you $125,000 to speak."

The president said, "Yeah, okay."

Now everybody is excited that this president is going to come to the 100 Club. That is, everyone except a Ford board member. When he heard about it, he said, "Who gave him the authorization to have that man come to the 100 Club? He is not coming! I'm putting my foot down. That guy is not coming to the 100 Club."

I think it was Dave Mondragon who was head of exhibitions at the time. He turned purple when he got that call: "That guy's not coming! You understand me?"

Dave says, "But, we already gave him the check."

"Who authorized the check?"

"I did."

"Who told you to?"

"I don't know." (He didn't want to say. Sometimes it's wise to take the heat and keep your mouth shut.)

Meanwhile, I'm at home sleeping. Around midnight, I get a call, "You've got to get me out of this! Get me out of this, Itsy."

"Out of what?"

"They don't want the president to come. This is a disaster. I sent him the check. He's going to come and now this higher-up won't let him come. We've got 100 dealers, this president is a Democrat. What if 80 of them are Republicans and 20 of them are Democrats? It will make us look stupid."

"Dave! Jesus Christ! Couldn't you wait until morning?" I groused.

The next day, I went to Hoot and said, "Hoot, we're in trouble.

We've got to do something. Will you call the president with me? We've got to tell him there was some controversy about it and let him keep the $125,000 check, but we have to have another speaker."

Ultimately, the president returned the check, being the person he is. We got another speaker, Bill O'Reilly. We kept it as quiet as we could and didn't let on what had happened. (It would have been a disaster if word had gotten out.) That was the worst.

Ford shares the road with Harley-Davidson

Here's another one that was almost as bad. It worked out well, but it was one of my biggest headaches -- the launch for Ford's 100th Anniversary.

Here's what happened: Ford came to me and said, "Its, we want to give 100 Harley-Davidsons to the top 100 dealers in the country and the Harleys would cost $18,000 each."

I said, "Why don't we have Bill Ford, Jr., sign the Harleys? 'Ford 100th Anniversary, Bill Ford Jr.'" Ford has been in a partnership with Harley Davidson since 2000, a partnership that had been going well with limited edition Ford F-150 Harley- Davidson trucks. Until now.

The Ford F-Series people called me and said, "They won't do it."

I said, "What are you talking about?"

"They're not going to do it. Harley-Davidson is not going to do it."

So I called Harley-Davidson and I asked them, "Are you nuts? We have an F-Series Harley and we're giving 100 Harleys at $18,000 a piece for our 100th anniversary."

"We're not doing it, Itsy! It's in our bylaws: A Harley only has a Harley logo. That's it! We're done. We're not doing it."

I said, "Get me the president of the company."

They did and so I asked him, "Are you crazy? You're going to tell us you're not going to do this?"

And he said, "No, we're not going to do it. We can't. It's in our bylaws."

I said, "Okay. So it's in your bylaws, then ship them to me without anything on them and I'll do them."

"You can't do that."

"You mean I can't do that because I'm giving you $1,800,000 of business? I can't do that? For that money, I can do anything I want. I'll get somebody to do it in Michigan to put the thing on."

"But our bylaws don't allow it."

"I don't give a shit what your bylaws say. This is Bill Ford, Jr., and you're going to do this."

Then I had an idea:

"Wait a minute! Who does your design on your Harleys? You take those Harleys over to him. I'll let him do it. He'll put the signatures and everything on it. And then it's ours."

He said, "I'll do it."

So we had Tom Celine, one of my best friends and a Harley-Davidson franchise owner, to get the Harleys shipped to him and watched over the whole project.

That was the biggest headache I've ever had on the job.

Fun with the Fords

I knew many members of the Ford family but I was closest to Buhl Ford. We were like brothers. He passed away in 2010 and I miss him terribly.

Buhl Ford's best friend was Al Strunk, the head of events at Ford, so I worked with him a lot. Of course, the three of us would go to lunch together a lot. We always had so much fun, he and Al Strunk and I. Buhl and Al liked to have an occasional social drink (within reason). As I never drink alcohol, I was always the designated driver. Al, who was the head of all events, was lucky he had Buhl for a friend. Al liked to live fast and loose. No one ever knew where he was.

I'd watch Buhl pick up his drink, tilt his head back, and swallow. Somehow he had a certain panache when he did so.

Once, I waited until just the right moment. Buhl was taking a drink and I said. "Can I ask a question Buhl?"

He nodded. I waited until the exact moment when the liquid got into his mouth:

"Do you get a company car?"

He spit his drink all over the table and laughed his ass off. He's a Ford -- of course he gets a company car!

How does the other half live?

All the Fords were expected to learn the business. When it was Benson Ford's turn, Jim Gwaltney, Ford's head of marketing, asked me to be his mentor. I did so without hesitation.

Up to that point, Benson had never gone to a Ford event, so he and I went to an introduction show at Walt Disney World in Orlando, where we were to show off our new products to potential customers.

We had some downtime and as the designated driver, I said, "What do you want to do, buddy? Anything you want to do, I'm your driver."

"Here's what I want to do," he said. "I want to see that snake thing in Kissimmee."

So we went and wandered around for a while. Benson knew quite a bit about snakes and talked to the trainers and we watched them milk the cobras. We had a good time, though a bit unusual.

When we left, I asked Benson what he wanted to do next.

"I want to go to the flea market." He had read the guide books and found a listing for a huge flea market nearby.

"Why do you want to go there?" I asked. After all, this guy had a $200 million company.

Turns out he and his wife collected commemorative glasses, so we wandered around the flea market for a couple of hours.

"Benson, it's a good thing you're dressed as you are," I told him, "so nobody knows you're a Ford. Otherwise, they'd want your autograph."

Around 2 p.m., I realized we had not eaten all day, so I asked Benson, "What would you like for lunch?"

"Dairy Queen."

So I went out to lunch with a member of the Ford family -- at Dairy Queen, of all places. (I'm not knocking Dairy Queen. They have good food and we had a great time that day. But that's just how unpretentious he was.)

My most embarrassing task

When you're working in corporate America, sometimes you are

asked to do things that are not exactly in the job description. Here's the most embarrassing thing I've ever been asked to handle. It concerns Al Strunk, head of events at Ford.

Al was in the process of getting a divorce. He had moved into an apartment but his wife was constantly after him because she wanted his money.

One day, I was in my office and I get a call from Al.

"Itsy! Itsy! Where are you? What are you doing?"

"I'm at the office." (Where else would I have been?)

"My wife is outside. She found out where I live and she's trying to get the money."

"So?"

"Be here at my apartment in Troy in 15 minutes. I'm going to put on a wig and a dress and nylons. When I walk out and get into your car, she won't know it's me."

"Al, are you playing with a full deck? Are you crazy?"

"You'd better come get me!" And he hung up.

So, I got in my car and drove to Al's apartment. His wife was there but she didn't see me. I pull around to the side of the building.

Al comes out. Sure enough, he's in drag. He turned his head so she couldn't see his face. He jumped in my car and we drove off.

So I drove around town with this man in very bad drag until the coast was clear. And that was the craziest, most embarrassing thing I did in corporate America. I always wondered if maybe I should have put up some money so he could see a good psychiatrist.

That's the way marketing goes. It could be the worst. It could be the best. That's the way it happens.

The Return of Itsy

I thought that was the end of me in marketing and corporate America. It didn't last long.

In 2005, I was retired for a year, playing golf at BallinIsles in Palm Springs, Florida, resting and going to see my kids at our

---

The Auto Downturn and Those Private Planes

I'm out of the auto industry now, but I still have a few things to say about it — especially the troubles the Big Three endured in recent years.

I'm especially furious at Congress and how it handled the GM and Chrysler bail-outs. Where does Congress get off criticizing corporate officials for using private planes?

If you're a president or a chairman or a vice chairman, you should go to meetings out of state in a private plane because you are leader of that company. If they flew commercial, what happens if the airline says, "I'm sorry ladies and gentlemen, we have mechanical difficulties, and our flight is delayed?" That executive misses a meeting that may have meant millions of dollars and jobs. Your company can't stop because an airline had a mechanical difficulty. You have work to do, you don't need the baby in the seat behind you screaming because of the change in air pressure.

You represent millions of people, so what is so terrible about going on a plane for $5,000 and stopping, having your meeting, and coming back home the same day, with time to see to other business? It gets the job done, it saves time and it leaves the chief officers free to see to their companies – a lot is riding on their success.

What happened during those congressional meetings in Washington? A lot of people said, "The Big Three should have gone bankrupt." Well I say, "No way, Jose!" The naysayers in Congress were just thinking of their own selves, trying to get headlines to make themselves look good. They were not thinking about the people who would have starved to death if the auto industry had gone under. That's a very selfish way to think.

Those congressmen said, "Well, don't come in a private plane." Why shouldn't they come in a private plane? They had no business saying that. The Big Three executives have businesses to run on top of all the hearings they had to go to in Washington. Do you want them to sit around waiting for a commercial flight?

The politicians said, "Well, you took a plane here." Yeah? The politicians took private planes themselves. They were trying to be rabble-rousers but they didn't know what they were talking about.

---

home in Charlevoix in northern Michigan. I was done. I didn't have to worry about anything.

"Boy oh boy! What a great feeling," I told myself.

One day, I run into Vinnie Johnson, one of the former Detroit Pistons. He said, "Its, I might need some help."

"With what?" I said.

"I'll call you. We'll have lunch."

Now Chuck Daly is one of the best friends I've ever had. I've even dedicated this book to him. Chuck and I were joined at the hip, we were that close. Chuck loved Vinnie, so I asked him what was up.

"I don't know what he wants to talk to you about," Chuck told me. "But help him out, he's a good guy. I really like him."

So I met with Vinnie and he said, "I bought AIREA, a furniture dealer for a company called Haworth. I'm having a little trouble with it. Maybe you can open some doors and get some businesses to accept my products."

I said, "Vinnie, I don't want to go back in business again. I just don't want to."

He said, "Its, would you do it for me? You know a lot of people. You know the bankers, the companies. You know Johnson Controls, you know Visteon, you know all of them."

So I said, "Okay, here's what I'm going to do. Give me an office. I'll take a commission. I'll be a salesman for you. I'll go to the banks and I'll go around and see if I can get business for you."

Well, I got him some business, but I could see that the company was not doing well. I could see it when I went to the facility. Vinnie is a wonderful businessman but I could see that everyone was whispering by the water coolers. It smelled like trouble.

"This company's got to get steady," I said.

Vinnie said, "I have to fire my president. I have to get another president. I want you to interview for the presidency."

"What!" I said. "Interview me for the presidency? I'm a salesman. I told you I don't want to do this. I don't know the first thing about furniture. No."

Vinnie said, "I'm paying my president over $240,000. I'll pay you $240,000 if my group thinks you're the right one for the job."

"It's not about the money, Vinnie," I said. "It's about my friendship for you. I don't want the $240,000. If I get it, I'll take $100,000, you take the $140,000 and pay some debts with it. What do you want me for?"

"Because you're a pit bull. You know how to get around people. You know what to say and you're charismatic." Vinnie said. "I have to have somebody go up to Holland, MI, and settle this thing. It's getting to the point where I could lose a lot of money."

So I go to the interview and the company's board says, "You're hired."

So I said, "Okay, but it's for one year. If I can't get it done in one year, I'm out of here. If I do get it done in one year, I'm out of here. That's it. I don't want more than one year. I'll do it as a friend. I'll take $100,000. I don't want the other stuff. I'll do it."

So Haworth starts calling Vinnie, "Who's this guy, Itsy Lieberman? You fired Mike Vaughan. Who the hell is this guy

> ### Watch your backside
> The real reason why the Big Three went bad was they didn't watch their backsides. The only one that did was Ford. You've got to watch your backside when you bring out product. As always, a lot of executives thought that this would never happen: GM, Chrysler going bankrupt. Only Ford sat there very calmly.
>
> I knew GM CEO Rick Wagner and I told him, "You know, you're going to go down. You've got to watch your backside. You're too complacent. You can't get complacent in the workforce or in sports or anything. The Tigers, Yankees don't win the Series every year. The Colts don't win the Super Bowl every year. They get complacent. You're getting complacent too and you can't let that happen."
>
> Look what's happening now. We're coming back. That's because the automakers stood together.

Lieberman? Nobody in furniture has ever heard of him."

Then they called me and said, "What do you know about furniture?"

I said, "I know I sit on it."

They said, "What else do you know?"

I said, "I don't know a thing about it."

They said, "Well, we want a meeting with you right away, the sooner the better. The board wants to meet with you and the CFO. We've got to get this thing done and have it done in an orderly way. We want you to come up next week."

So I said, "Okay, I'll come up next week."

In the meantime, I learned a lot about the furniture industry and the company I was dealing with. I learned that Haworth had a lot more control over AIREA than I had thought. For a variety of reasons, it looked like they set my friend Vinnie up to fail, forcing him to hire people to hurt the AIREA franchise. Why? I don't know. These things happen in business.

Before I left for the meeting, I told Vinnie, "Vinnie, I don't want you coming here with me. I love you too much. Because I do, let me take the hit. You might get whacked at. I don't want that to happen. Let me handle it. You gave me the responsibility."

I had a team of AIREA people coming with me and I told them that I was going to be the quietest person there and this was all going to be very professional. "Just follow my lead," I told them. "Follow my lead. I've got the blueprint. Follow my lead."

On the day of the meeting, I knew what I was going to do. I went there in my striped suit and my white shirt and tie. (In corporate America, there was never a day when I didn't go with my white starched shirt, a corporate suit, shined shoes and a puff in my pocket. I even modeled in a couple of magazines.) I walked in and greeted everyone with, "Good to see you, sir. Good to see you, ma'am."

We went into the boardroom. In comes the CFO with his three henchmen and his analyst.

I introduced myself, "I'm Itsy Lieberman, and I'm here to represent AIREA. I'm taking Mike Vaughan's job. I'll tell you what I know about furniture – nothing. I don't know about furniture and I don't care that I don't know about furniture. I came here because I know about business. I've got business ethics. I want to lead this thing right now. What are you going to do about it?"

"What am I going to do about it?" the CFO sputters. "What am I going to do about it? What are you going to do about it? He owes a ton of money here. We're upside down. Here's your balance sheet. Look at it. We're upside down. The company owes more than it's worth!"

"Yeah? We are upside down. So what are you going to do about it? I was in corporate America for years and I know what's going on. It's a set up. Who gave AIREA Mike Vaughan to run the business? Who? Where did he come from? Haworth put him there on purpose to sink the company. And now we have to clean up the mess."

It got pretty hot in there. I said, "I'm not going to stay here for an hour, because I don't want to unless we get something done here. I'm leaving this room with all of my people now for a half hour. And when I get back, you're going to tell me what you're going to do about it."

The CFO said, "What do you want me to do about it?"

I said, "I want half of that debt wiped out. I want to restructure the business. I want credit and we'll go from there. Whatever you want, it's your call. Now, I'm taking my team out for coffee."

I got up to leave, followed by my entourage. We had some coffee and came back to the board room. We walked in, and I said, "What's your answer?"

"We're going to do it."

"Fine, what are the terms?"

"We'll take off half the debt."

"Okay. Restructure us?"

"Yeah."

"Credit?"

"Yes."

We got all of it. We walked out. The group told me, "What just happened in there? Are you out of your mind? You were like a trial lawyer. We've never seen anyone so passionate."

The second best thing that ever happened to me in corporate America happened next. I said to the CFO, "Thanks. I appreciate it. The board said we'll get it done. But why did you do it? You didn't have to do this. He's got a $4.5 million debt and you did all this. Why?"

"Itsy, I had 10 of my people go to Ford, Chrysler, GM," he said. "We checked out where you live, who you are. We asked the big power brokers in Michigan. Every one of them said, 'You'll never beat him. That guy will come after you. He'll tell the truth and you will not beat him. He is so powerful. He knows so many people that would jump in his corner. You don't want to get involved in that. Settle with him or you'll lose your shirt."

When he said that, I couldn't believe it. Who's this guy, Itsy Lieberman?

So we won and we settled. The company is still in business. Vinnie and I are still friends. I go there every so often to say hello to Yolanda and Mark and the rest. But I don't want anything to do with corporate America again. It was a great run. I've been happy. All I can say is thanks.

A special tribute to a special friend

I couldn't close this chapter on my life in corporate America without talking about the guy who I have the most love for. His name is Hoot McInerney. He is an icon in the auto industry. He had 29 dealerships at one time. He sold them, bought them. He had his own plane. The guy treated me like royalty. He took me to the Bob Hope to play golf. He took me to California whenever he went. He took me to Las Vegas. He took me to New York. He's one of my greatest friends. I enjoy his company so much.

Hoot McInerney

If you go to any dealer in the United States of America and ask them, "Did you know Hoot McInerney?" you will see them get a big smile on their faces. He is America's automobile guru and nobody will tell you otherwise. He knows what he's doing. He's a fun guy. He's given more to charity than anyone I know. That guy is a man's man. I hope someday that there's a statue in Downtown Detroit for Hoot McInerney.

I've got a couple of funny stories about Hoot that I've got to share.

How Hoot treats his friends

One day, Hoot calls me and says, "Its, it's the last golf event at the Desert Inn owned by Steve Wynn. They're tearing it down. Let's go. We'll play."

I said, "You want me to go?"

He said, "Yeah. Let's go. We'll get on the jet and leave at 2 p.m. and go to Las Vegas." And so we did.

When we land in Vegas, Hoot has a limousine waiting for us as always. He said, "Its, I'm staying at the MGM. There's a Rolls Royce in the garage and a 5,000-square-foot suite. You're staying at the Bellagio."

"I'm not staying with you?"

"No. You're staying in a 4,000-square-foot suite at the Bellagio. Tonight we're going to dinner. We're going over the Desert Inn to check out who we're playing tomorrow. By the way, there's a birthday party for Shaquille O'Neal."

This is all really impressive but it wasn't me.

I said, "I don't want to meet him. I don't care about meeting those people. I don't care about Shaquille O'Neal, Hoot. I came here with you, you're my buddy. I don't care about those people."

Hoot was paying and I was his guest and he wasn't having any of it. So we went to the Desert Inn and saw all the celebrities. As part of the festivities, there was a raffle so we bought tickets. All the celebrities are there from all over the world.

After we find out our arrangements for the next day's tournament, I go back to my suite, which was jaw-droppingly beautiful. It had every amenity you could think of. They even sent somebody up to cut my hair. With tongue firmly in cheek, I ask, "Isn't there a bigger suite than this?"

They said, "Sir, your suite is 4,800 square feet."

"Oh, okay," I said. I was being very facetious. This was the biggest room I'd ever had in my life.

We made an early night of it because we had an early tee time to beat the heat of the day in Las Vegas. Hoot picked me up in the limousine the next day.

"How'd you like the suite?" he asked me.

"Bah, it stunk," I said.

He laughed, "Yeah, it stunk all right."

"I've never been in suite like that," I said. "I'd never be in a suite like that, it's only because it's your money and your plane. Thanks."

He said, "That's okay. Now, we're going to tee off at 7 o'clock and then we're going to have lunch with Steve Wynn and Arnold Schwarzenegger."

"What?!"

"We're having lunch with Wynn and Arnold Schwarzenegger today."

So we play and have lunch with Schwarzenegger and Wynn, who built a lot of the resorts on the Las Vegas Strip and was one of the richest men in the world.

Now, I had a German shepherd, Onyx. I loved but I had to put down. I really missed Onyx, a beautiful dog.

As it happens, Steve Wynn also had a German shepherd. Chuck Daly had told me, "If you want a German shepherd, go to the guy who got Steve Wynn his German shepherd." So Steve and I start to talk about German Shepherds. Nobody else is talking. Arnold Schwarzenegger and Hoot are not talking. It's just me and one of the most powerful men in Vegas talking about dogs, of all things.

Wynn said, "You go to this guy and you tell him that you want a German shepherd and I will send my private plane to pick you and that dog up. But I'm not picking you up alone. That dog has got to come with you."

(Later on, in the Family Room chapter, I'll tell you all about getting my new German shepherd.)

Now Arnold Schwarzenegger was there because he's big, broad, and muscular. GM thought was just the guy to be the spokesman for the Hummer. So we talked and were having a nice time.

Hoot says, "They're having a shoot out here in a few minutes. I don't want to stay for that, Itsy. Let's go."

We get in the limousine and head on out of the lot. The guy at the gate says, "Is there an Itsy Lieberman in this limousine?"

I said, "Yes sir. It's me."

He said, "You won the Hummer."

I said, "Who put you up to this and how much money did they give you to do it?" It had to be a joke but I wasn't getting it.

CHAPTER 2

"Nobody. You've got to turn back. You. Won. The. Hummer."

Sigh. We go back. The shoot out is over. We just make it back in time. Elaine Wynn, Steve's then-wife, was at the podium. When she sees me, she announces, "Here comes the winner of the Hummer! Itsyyyy Liebermannnnn!"

So, I had to go up on stage. All these people are there and I have to make a speech and everything. I said, "I'm passionate about where I come from and I'm a Motown Motowner. We're Hockeytown USA. We're Baseball USA. We're Basketball USA. We have a little problem with football, but it'll come back. I'm proud to be from the Motor Capital of the World. Thank you so much for this. I thank my host, Hoot, for bringing me out here. He's always been a good friend. I'm really elated to have won the Hummer."

Arnold Schwarzenegger and I took 50 pictures together. "Its, good to see you," he says in his strong Austrian accent.

We finally leave and get past the guard shack. While we're driving down the street, I finally got a chance to say what's been on my mind:

"Hoot, I can't take the Hummer. I work for Ford."

Hoot said, "Ohh!" He realized the mess I was in.

Then I said, "Hey Hoot! You brought me here, didn't you? You paid for the gas, didn't you? You paid for that 'cheap' suite, didn't you? We're going to gamble tonight, aren't we?"

"Yeah."

"Tell you what: Sell the Hummer and we'll split the proceeds."

And that's what we did. I got $24,000. He got $24,000. On top of a luxury trip, rubbing elbows with the stars, we both cleared $24,000. Hoot never forgot that.

Isn't that a great story?

Another Hoot story

Hoot is struggling right now at his age. I hope he lives another 100 years because he was so good to me. John Cuter, Hoot's right-hand man, has been good to me, too – I hope they erect a statue in his honor. He's been with Hoot for 50 years. He stays at his house, run his errands and so on. John, I tip my hat to you for being such a great friend to my friend.

I tip my hat also to Doctor Christopher Chay, Hoot's doctor. I thank you so much for being in Hoot's corner. I tip my hat to Jack Christian for being in his corner. I hope he lives forever.

I've got to tell you another very, very funny story. This is a classic.

John Cuter called me and said, "Its, I'm at the hospital with Hoot and he's not doing very well."

I went to the hospital and took Hoot by the hand and squeezed it. John was at my side as I said, "Hoot, please don't die on me. Please don't die on me. Please don't die on me."

Hoot opened his eyes and looked at me and said, "Why?"

John Cuter said, "Because then I'd have to fly commercial."

Hoot laughed his ass off. He came around and recovered just fine. After all – Hoot's Hoot.

My corporate life is over. I took my money and said, "I'm not coming back. It's always the same. I got out when the money was good."

I was lucky to have good people with me. I happened to be at the right time and the right place. I'm very blessed to be in that era. I want to thank everyone for being so good to me.

Lessons from the Boardroom

Listen

Don't make rash decisions

Don't believe everything you hear.

Be a gentleman (or a lady).

Don't backstab people.

Work hard.

Work Smart.

You'll win.

Remember, you're part of a team. I've been fortunate to have a great team: George Alteri, my "lieutenant"; Luann Shaw, who took on GM and Detroit Diesel; Mel Goulson, who took on Chrysler and Mopar and should have been on television because he was so funny. Thank you for being my team and making me look good. You deserve all the credit.

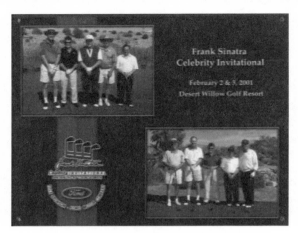

Itsy at the Frank Sinatra Celebrity
Invitational, 2001

CHAPTER III
T·H·R·E·E

THE CLUB ROOM

"Never get into a pissing contest with a skunk."

▶ ERWIN "ITSY" LIEBERMAN

If you've had any dealings with corporate America, undoubtedly you've heard that many deals are not made in the board room. They're made on the golf course or the club house.

That's certainly true of marketing in the auto industry. Golf was a very important part of my professional life. I'm out of that arena, but the golf course is still my home away from home. Especially Red Run Golf Club in Royal Oak.

I learned about Red Run back in 1987 when I was calling on the auto companies. I was chairman and CEO of PVL and I had salesmen going to the Big Three. They always came back and said, "They want to play golf. We need a golf club."

I don't play golf, not really, but I could see they were right, so I said, "Okay, we'll get a golf club."

I would go to Pontiac, I'd go to Buick, I'd go to Chrysler and I'd go to Ford. They all told me they wanted a golf club, too. They wanted to play on the weekend and after 4 p.m. to play nine holes.

So I went looking for a golf club. I went to Franklin Hills Country Club. I went to Knollwood and Tam O'Shanter – all the best golf clubs in the Detroit area. (They were also golf courses that I knew accepted Jews as members.) I went back to the Big Three and asked them which of those three courses they wanted.

All of them said, "Red Run."

I said, "Why?" It was only a half mile from my home and it didn't seem to me to be anything special. The other courses were in the Birmingham/Bloomfield Hills area, where most of the auto executives lived.

"That club is superb, it's in great shape," they said. But the real story was, "When we're invited to Red Run, there are more crazies at the men's grill than you can shake a stick at."

"But I'm Jewish," I said. "I don't know if I can get into Red Run. I know a lot of people there but they may say, 'We don't want him.'"

Still they said, "Red Run."

Frank Gallagher, one of my very best friends who played eight years for the Detroit Lions, played at Red Run. So I went to him.

"Frank, all of my clients want to get a golf course and they all want Red Run," I said. "Do you think I can get in?"

Then I went to Don Brooks, the course champion, and said, "Don, do you think I can get in? I'm Jewish. Has there ever been a Jew there other than me?"

Joe Costello, Marty Cowens, Chuck Daley, Joe Teramova, & Itsy

"Well there was one, but he was only there about a year." Donny said. "Great," I thought, but still, if that's what my clients wanted, I'd better give it a try.

"Do I have a chance?" I asked both of them.

"Itsy, you will get in hands down," Frank and Donny both said. "Don't worry about it."

They were right, I needn't have worried. I got in. There should be a sit-com about Red Run. We have every ethnicity in the world. We have Serbians, Albanians, Lebanese, Jewish people, Italians, Armenians, African-Americans. And every one of them gets along. It's an amazing melting pot of golf. There's no other golf club in the United States that is such a melting pot. They get along and they love each other, but they're a little off-kilter.

Red Run has the greatest guys I've ever met in my life. I'd love to mention them all by name. If I miss a name, I'm sorry but I can't put 340 names in a book.

If you go to Red Run, everyone is so nice to each other and so crazy. There are so many characters there, it's unbelievable, but they are great characters. I'm starting my 25th year at Red run and I saw a lot there. I've had a million laughs there. I call it the Funny Farm. They asked me to run for the board several times but I've always said no because I love Red Run. If I was on the board, I might have enemies and I don't want to get into the politics. Red Run is my home and I like it.

If you go on the course, you'll see Mike Lucci, Lew Price, John Fayad, Dan Hucul and about 18 other foursomes and every one of them is playing for a certain amount of money. They will never, ever turn away a person saying, "I'm going to play you for this amount of money." They'll say, "Let's get it on."

If you ever were asked to go to dinner with Jim Yarema or Hank Kinzey, you'd better not bring your wallet because those two guys are the most gracious guys I've ever met in my life. They'll fight you for the bill, believe it. Hank is the type of person everyone wants to work for and work with. The guy has a heart of platinum – I've never seen a person who is so helpful to everybody.

Jim Yarema has a great son, Dave, who is now about 40 and is a member of Red Run too. Dave is confident, smart, the most level-headed guy I've ever met. I enjoy being in his company. He was All-State at Brother Rice and holds many passing records at Brother Rice and at Michigan State. (I love watching Dave walking down the hall with Dave Zelmanski, who played baseball at Wayne State, so it's MSU and Wayne State – rival schools – side by side. He was even given a tryout by the Green Bay Packers.) Jim, you've really raised a tremendous son. Dave, be as proud of your father as your father is proud of you.

All three of them -- Jim, Dave and Hank Kinzey -- are perfect gentlemen in the best sense of the word. I feel the same way about Ray Lope, who was a great basketball player at St. Francis. Whenever he comes into the room at Red Run, I can't help but think, "There comes a perfect gentleman."

I can't forget to mention Rob Ledbetter. He's my twin since we were both born on September 26. It doesn't matter if we were born in different years. It also doesn't matter that I'm 5 foot 6 and 170 lbs and he's 6 foot 8 and 340 lbs -- we're twins. We're a real Mutt and Jeff team.

Crazy Caddy

Pat McGaughey has some great stories about the antics at Red Run. One of the best concerns a caddy, who shall remain nameless.

One Thursday, Royal Oak police officers spotted a golf cart driving along 12 Mile Road. Because golf carts are not "street legal," they pulled the driver over. It seems one of our caddies had gotten hungry and was driving over to the local pizzeria to pick up the pizza he had ordered. The caddy took the long way around – he had driven the carts down Red Run's range road, through a park and a cemetery to get his food.

As if that weren't bad enough, of all the carts the caddy could have "borrowed," he took the one holding the golf bags of two of the area's most prominent judges – and the bags were impounded as evidence.

Pat had to argue with the police, "We don't need the cart, but we need those clubs." The police were kind enough to allow Red Run to substitute another set of clubs so the judges could have theirs back.

Another of my buddies is Mark Hogan, who was with Magna. He's a great guy and I would always joke with him so he wouldn't be so serious. (His kids went to Brother Rice High School, a rival of Detroit Country Day, so I would rib him about that.)

Our starter, Pat McGaughey, has been there about 40 years. He and his assistant Keith are great. Our greens keeper Gary Thommes has been there the same amount of time. The course is always in top shape. Wally, our pro, and Steve, Brian, and Mark are so helpful.

Whenever I bring people to Red Run, they rave about the course. It's all thanks to its people: General Manager Derek Jacques, Board President Pat DeSmet and the rest of the people on the board of directors, along with all the course staff — John the dining room manager, Warren Batchelor who runs the locker room, Scott the trainer, Natalie the catering manager, Cheryl the receptionist, Ed the chef, Cedric the dining room captain and the rest of the dining room staff -- Eddie, George, Russ, Robby, Ted, Scott, Mike, Johnny, Chris, Cherle, Jake — even the two valets and the accounting staff upstairs do a great job. Everyone is always so poised and Red Run is so blessed to have you. We're one big family.

I have special affection for Mike who serves my water in the Men's Grille, and Cheryl the receptionist. When Cheryl answers the phone with her cheery, "Red Run," I always ask for "Day Care Center."

If you go to the gin table, watch out. You'll find Red Zone Nick Mondella, a WWII hero, who is the most colorful person you'll ever meet. His personality is unbelievable. You've got

---

Anything can happen at Red Run

I'm not saying the folks at Red Run cheat but some of them have been known to bend the truth a little. Pat McGaughey tells the story of one lawyer who wasn't especially good at it: The lawyer had been caught cheating by kicking his ball to a better location. He was summoned before the Red Run Board of Directors for disciplinary action but he was a little confused.

"Which hole?" he asked. "The second or the 15th?"

Pat also remembers caddying for Gary Bergman, formerly of the Detroit Red Wings. "He gave a mighty blast on the 11th hole that, when the ball landed, the interior rubber bands were flying off in all directions," Pat said. "I said to him, 'Let's see you putt that one.'"

---

everybody yelling at each other in a gin game and swearing and so on.

Everyone I've ever taken to Red Run loves it. I took a pro from BallanIsles country club to Red Run, then to Oakland Hills.

"Which one did you like better, Johnny?" I asked him as we finished a round and were heading into the club house.

"Red Run," he said.

"Listen John, at Red Run, within 20 minutes after you play golf, they're going to sit down for lunch, and there's going to be an argument at the gin table. So don't get crazy."

I was right. Within 20 minutes, there was an argument. But I love Red Run.

We've lost a lot of good people -- some of my friends. Good friends like Tom Roncelli, Leo Kargol; so many good people, including the chairman of the board of Red Run, Mike Dorian. There will never be another Mike Dorian.

Another great member we've lost was Ron Kramer, who was the greatest athlete ever to play in the state of Michigan. Nobody was better than Ron Kramer: Green Bay Packer, All Pro, All-American at Michigan in basketball, football, and track. He's in all the Michigan sports hall of fames. Ron, I miss you.

Another Red Run friend whom I miss very much is Naizi Bardha. He was a character's character. He and his brothers, Agim and Eric, are great Albanians. He was part of the classic foursome with Marv Schemerhorn, Jerry "Looney Tunes" Linderberg, and Nick "Red Zone" Mondella. When they were on the course, there'd be so much arguing we always said they should have put on armor first. Naizi hit more divots at Red

Run over three years than were hit at any other golf course. I miss him terribly.

What Red Run is all about

I want to tell a story that will tug at your heartstrings and shows what Red Run was all about. There was a guy named Ed Kasparian, who I often played gin with.

My embarrassing 15 minutes of fame

Ron Kramer was partially responsible for my most embarrassing moment.

One evening in December 1999, Ron Kramer and Joe Schmidt (former player and coach of the Lions) were guests on Bob Hines radio program. (I didn't know it.) They were talking about the greatest athletes of the 20th century. They were working from a list of about 20 athletes, like Jim Thorpe, Joe DiMaggio, Cassius Clay, and so on.

"Which of these guys was the greatest?" Bob asked Joe.

"He's not on the list," Joe said. "The greatest athlete was Itsy Lieberman."

"I've never heard of him," Bob said.

"Oh Itsy was a tremendous athlete," Joe said. "He was at Wayne State. He started out at St. Ladislaus." (Yeah right, an obviously Jewish name like Itsy Lieberman, at a Catholic school.)

Joe said this on purpose to get at me. Ron played along. "I agree with Joe. Itsy was a superstar."

I was at home relaxing when out of the blue I started getting phone calls. There must have been 70 of them in an hour.

"Itsy! You're on the radio! They said you were the top athlete of the century!"

Oy Gevalt!

Ed Kasparian had a Ford dealership, but he liked to gamble, like all the other guys at Red Run. He lost his dealership because of it. He was done and was really down and out.

"Ed, listen," I told him. "You're only a half mile from me at Red Run. I love you: we play gin together. I don't want you to not have any money. I'll hire you and pay you. I'll give you a car allowance and a salary."

Ed was so gracious. We'd go to lunch every day at Red Run. He was a great friend of mine.

One day a call came that his daughter had to have an operation. His daughter called Lou Dorian, Mike's wife. We found out the operation would cost $25,000. Ed didn't have any health insurance or money.

As it happens, we knew Eddie's 70th birthday was coming up. We said, "Ed, we're taking you to Café Cortina for your birthday."

Thirty-three of us were there with our wives, with Eddie and some other people. First, Mike Dorian got up and spoke. Then, Mike Lucci got up and said, "Ed, we got you the best golf shoes we could find that Bally makes. You're a dapper dresser, you always wear the best. We want to give you these shoes."

Mike gave him the shoe box. Eddie opened it. Inside was $33,000. Each of us had given $1,000 to help Ed with his daughter.

Eddie and his wife couldn't stop crying. Thanks to you guys: Tom Bosbous, Lew Price, Mike Lucci, Tony Versaci, Roger Denha, the Robinson family, Mike Dorian, and 28 others.

I'm not really a golfer so I've got to recognize all my gin-playing cronies: Phil Keila, Ron Paske, Bert DiStefano, Linus, Louie Comaianni, Ted Derwa, Charles DeVito, Art Shaw, Mike Santi, and Kerry Kennedy. You're what Red Run is all about. (Thanks to all of you. But if you still owe me any money, put it in my locker. If I missed anyone, know I love Red Run. It's like having another family.)

The surgery was a success by the way. Eddie is long gone now, but we still remember him.

Itsy gets even

That's not to say we can't have a little fun at each other's expense, however. I remember one time I was playing gin with Mike Dorian, Red Zone Nick, and Jerry "Loony Tunes" Linderberg.

Mike lit into me after one game, "Geez Its! Why did you do that? You knew the queen was hot, you Hebe!"

"I didn't realize an Armenian could think," I shot back.

As much as Red Run is a real melting pot, I didn't like Dorian calling me a "Hebe." I wanted to get back at him, but I waited until the time was right.

About a half-dozen games later, I had my chance.

"Mike, listen," I told him. "I've been noticing, you really look pale. You feeling all right?"

"What are you talking about?" he scoffed.

"Your face is really pale and your cheeks, it's like they're jaundiced or something."

"Shut up, Itsy," Mike said.

"Mike, I'm not a doctor, but I'm telling you, I had a friend who looked like you do and it turned out he had *rachmonis*. He almost died. He was in the hospital 2 ½ weeks."

"Itsy, you're an idiot," Mike said. "Let's play cards."

"All right, but don't say I didn't warn you."

At the end of the hand, Mike gets up to use the men's room. I kind of snuck in behind him and saw him looking at his face in the mirror. I kept warning him but he kept calling me an idiot.

A while later, after we had all gone home, I got a phone call. It was Mike Dorian.

"Itsy, I'm at the doctor's office," he said. "Tell the doctor what this thing was you told me about."

I told the doctor about my friend's *rachmonis*.

"I've never heard of it," the doctor said.

"Well, you call my doctor. His name is Leroy Newman. Ask him. He'll tell you."

Well, Mike's doctor called Dr. Newman, who gave him the real diagnosis. "You have been taken by one of the greatest pranksters around."

You see, *rochmanis* is a Yiddish word. It means "pity."

The next time Mike came into the men's grill at Red Run, he shook me around till I thought my head would spin. He really went berserk.

Ain't I a stinker?

As you can see we're all pretty playful here. One guy who is a real character's character is Wally Baker. I've known him from the first day I came to Red Run.

If there's one thing I know about Wally is that he hates losing. I know that because he always has to keep score—gin or golf.

Chi Chi Rodriguez, Itsy, and the McInernys

Wally and I belong to the 500 club, along with John

Aska, Jerry McWilliams, and Nick Mondella. We're called the 500 Club because when we play golf, we always shoot in the 100s! John always rides with Wally to check on the scores.

I love to get Wally in one of my practical jokes. Here's one of my better tricks.

One Saturday morning, I stopped for breakfast at Red Run on my way to a doctor's appointment. As I was leaving, I saw Wally's golf bag in the rack by the door. I looked around but didn't see anyone, so I grabbed the bag and ran to my locker where I emptied all his golf balls. Then I snuck over to the practice range and filled his golf bag with range balls. After carefully replacing his golf bag in the rack, I went on my way to the doctor's.

When I came back that afternoon, John Aska told me that Wally had gone nuts. He didn't need to tell me that – Wally was glaring at me, just fuming.

"Wally! What's wrong?" I said, playing innocent.

"You know what happened," he said.

When Wally had gone out on the course, he took out a ball. Right away, he could tell something wasn't right. (Range balls don't fly nearly as far as regular golf balls.)

He took out another ball from his bag. Again, he could tell something was wrong. He went to his bag for a third time – again, the ball was no good.

Because Wally didn't know I had stashed his golf balls in my locker, he had to buy a dozen golf balls. He didn't appreciate that. Sorry Wally.

Someone else gets his 15 minutes of fame

Another time, I made Wally famous.

Several years ago, we were having lunch and Jerry Biebuyck (a guy I'd trust with my life) said, "Let's go to a Tiger's game."

So I got four tickets for Jerry, Bill Kehoe, Wally, and me. At the time the Detroit Tigers were still playing at Tiger Stadium at Michigan and Trumbull. I was friends with Gary DeVito, the executive vice president of the Tigers at the time, so we got great tickets – 2nd row box seats.

We were having a ball. Then in the seventh inning, I looked up.

"Oh my God! Look at the scoreboard, guys!"

The sign read, "The Detroit Tigers welcome Auburn University's Star Running Back, Wally Baker!"

The rest of us couldn't stop laughing – but not Wally: "My God! You've made a fool of me!" he said. "It's a full house. Every seat is full!"

"Wally, chill out! Not one person here knows who you are!"

That did it. Wally sat back down. "Yeah. I guess you're right. No one does know who I am." We laughed about it the whole way home.

Of course, we know who Wally is: Most guys call him the Edger, but I call him Porky. He never cheats – he just can't count. Wally, thank you for being who you are and part of the Funny Farm.

Lessons from the Club Room

Never play gin with Red Zone Nick Mondella.

Never try to top Itsy Lieberman in practical jokes.

Never go to a synagogue on Sunday.

CHAPTER
F·O·U·R

IV

THE WORKOUT ROOM

"You don't know what you don't know."

▶ ERWIN "ITSY" LIEBERMAN

*Itsy with Kyle
Vanden Bosch*

I've been teaching Chi exercises for 38 years. I've had a ball doing it. I'm passionate about what I do. I love people and I want to put a smile on their faces and make them feel good about themselves.

My career in the workout room started in the early 1970s. That's when karate became a big thing.

"You know, I'm going to try karate," I said. "It's good exercise. I'm not a fighter but it looks interesting."

I went to a dojo (a martial arts school) at 8 Mile and Van Dyke, one of the worst areas of Detroit. Karate was just starting to take off so there just weren't that many dojos around yet.

I progressed pretty steadily, going from my white belt to my yellow to my green in Korean karate, Tang Soo Do. In 1974, Itsy got his black belt. I made a lot of friends in the meantime. I was on the board of directors.

I salute Dave Priam and Dave Prue for starting the K-1 dojo. If you want two role models, go to David Priam and Dave Prue. At one point, we won the world championship: Detroit actually beat California for the world championships. That's how good we were.

In the early 1970s, you were not allowed to actually hit people in martial arts. The idea was to mimic attacking and defending yourself without actually touching your opponent. If you threw a punch and if you hit a guy, you'd get a point that counted against you. It's all about control. You know you could hit him, but you have to have control.

CHAPTER 4

One day during the black belt session on Monday night, something happened. David Priam brought in the all-time Tang Soo Do champion from Korea, a Mr. Lee. He was my size but you'd never want to mess with him. He became the face of Tang Soo Do.

Mr. Lee had a rule, "If you hit somebody, and I hear about it, you're going to get it."

One day, a guy named Chuck Latimer was sparring with me. He threw a reverse spin kick and kicked me in the temple. I went down and I was out for about five minutes. When I came around I said, "What did you do that for?"

> **Chuck Norris**
> One weekend the two Daves (Priam and Prue) brought in Chuck Norris. Four of us -- the two Daves, Wilson Highsaw, and I --took Chuck to the Premier Center to see Loretta Lynn and Roy Clark perform. They had Chuck stand up to be recognized and, because I knew the owners of the Premier Center pretty well, I was able to take him backstage to meet Loretta Lynn and Roy Clark. (Even if I hadn't known the owners, who would dare say no to Chuck Norris?)
> Chuck was a great guy, I really enjoyed him.

"I'm going for the championships," was Chuck's excuse. He didn't want to hold anything back.

I was the one who held back. I waited. During a black belt session we would switch partners so we can learn from each one. I waited until Chuck came around as my partner again. I saw Mr. Lee's back was to me. This was my chance.

"Ahh! Goddammit! Geez, he hit me! Shit! Ohhh! God Almighty…" I dropped to the ground and started rolling around.

Mr. Lee turned around and saw me. He came over and beat the shit out of Latimer.

After I got my black belt, I taught at the dojo for eight years.

A Dinner to Remember

One day, the two Daves told me, "We're going to Herbie Chen's for dinner tonight. He invited us over." Herbie lived near Wayne State University in Detroit, another really tough area.

"Great! Tell me me about it tomorrow," I said.

The next day at the dojo, I asked them, "How'd it go?" I asked.

"You'll never believe it," they said. They both looked upset, which is saying a lot for two martial arts masters.

"What happened?"

"We walk into his house and there's white powder everywhere. His whole house was covered with it – every single surface!"

"What?" I said. "Why?"

"His pet boa constrictor was loose," they said, "and he always finds it when he puts white powder over everything. We could barely eat because anytime we'd see anything out the corner of our eyes, we'd hit the ceiling."

"I told you he was off-kilter," I said through my laughter.

Herbie didn't find the snake until the next day.

Even though I liked karate very much, I got out after teaching for eight years because it had changed to full-contact karate. I had my wife, my kids, and my job to think about. I was 30 years old and had a lot of responsibilities. Why would I want to risk getting hurt? So I got out. I needed something to replace karate, which I had thoroughly enjoyed, but what?

I was in Las Vegas and still pondering what I was going to do. I saw an Asian guy doing these exercises, waving his arms through the air and moving in slow motion. "Sir, what are you doing?" I asked him.

"I'm doing my Chi exercises," he said. He started talking about chi qong and tai chi.

"I was a black belt in karate," I said. "Are they like karate?"

"Oh no, no, no," he said. He explained a little bit more and really got me interested.

When I got back to Michigan, I started reading books and finding out all about this art form. Chi or tai chi is composed of "forms," or series of movements. There are hundreds of such forms. You've probably seen tai chi being performed – a group of people performing identical movements at a slow, flowing pace. It's been sometimes called "meditation in motion."

I got an instructor who taught Chi exercises. I started to love it. Chi means "life's energy." The two most important things in life's energy are flexibility and agility so those are what tai chi promotes. They are crucial to the aging process.

It's only recently that I finally discovered why I like Chi so much. It's because the moves are so similar to those of animals. I've always been fascinated with animals – how they move, how they act. So many Chi movements are named for animals – "Cow Jumping Over the Moon, "Punching the Tiger's Eye," and so on.

I see that especially whenever I work with kids. Whenever I teach them, I start by saying, "Okay, we're going to play animals, kids. Let's be a snake. How does a giraffe walk?" I make them follow me and imitate me and they have a ball. That's why they get interested in Chi.

I like Chi because it's soft. I learned to focus on my breathing. I like the terminology and the moves. How can you not like an exercise called "Drunken Monkey?" It was really interesting and I ended up teaching it and still do today, 38 years later. In the 1980s I had my own show on Metro-Vision, a local cable service.

I did the show alone for about two to three years, then I brought on a guy named Wing Hong, who was from China. He used to own the Wing Hong restaurants where I used to go for Chinese food.

On the show it was like Laurel and Hardy or Abbott and Costello. I was the joker and Wing Hong was the straight man.

One day, Wing came to the studio in his *gi*, the Asian-style uniform for doing the exercises. I said, "Wing, are you playing with a full deck of cards today?"

"What do you mean?" he asked.

"You have your *gi* on but you're in your work shoes, not your slippers."

"Arrgh! I forgot."

"What are you going to do? We're going on television."

"I'll just take off my shoes."

(Although tai chi is performed very slowly, it's usually not a good idea to do the exercises in bare feet because of all the turning and shifting of weight. Besides, Itsy the prankster had an idea.)

"No. No. We're going in a half hour. You're not taking off your shoes. Don't worry about it. Nothing's going to happen. I'll make sure the crew doesn't show you with your shoes on."

He said, "Okay. Thank you, Itsy."

So we taped as usual. Then, when we had about 10 minutes left, I said, "You know, you sometimes have to rely on your memory and breathing gives you great memory. I'll show you how well it works. Look at Wing Hong's shoes. Wing, are you playing with a full deck today? Didn't you know you have your shoes on?"

The camera pulled back to show off Wing Hong's shoes.

Wing Hong sputtered, "You...you told me you weren't going to show them!"

I looked at him, so innocently, "I didn't say any such thing."

We all broke up, laughing and laughing.

An unexpected reward

I like teaching and I enjoy taping the television show but sometimes it can feel isolating. You generally have no way of knowing if anyone is even watching.

One day, this lady came in when I was taping on Metro vision. We taped on Saturday at 8:30 in the morning. She comes in and says, "Are you Itsy?"

"Yes, I am."

"I love you."

"You love me?" (I couldn't see where this was going. I'm not exactly George Clooney or Brad Pitt.)

"And my friends love you. I had to come here and tell you this."

"Why?"

"I have Lyme disease and five of my friends do, too. We watch you every time. You have made me so happy because I'm getting better."

I grabbed her in a hug and she kissed me. "I'll be there for you all the way," I said. "And for the other people."

By this time I was crying, it was so gratifying.

I was on Peter Nielsen's show for about four years. I'd do the Chi exercises of the month. Eventually I wanted to have my own studio. My wife's friend, Linda, was a yoga instructor and she wanted to have her own studio, too, so we decided to team up.

"Okay, Linda, we'll be partners," I said.

Our studio, Yoga Chi, was in downtown Birmingham, across

Itsy and Vivian with General Colin Powell

from the Townsend Hotel. We had a lot of celebrities come in: Britney Spears came in and so did a lot of directors and athletes.

I taught tai chi in the morning and in the evenings. We had the studio for eight years and then we sold it to Yoga Shelter. Linda wanted to do more private clients and she was also a masseuse, so I understood.

I did this thing called The Cup Cup Foo Walk. Every day at 7 a.m. we'd do our Chi exercises, and then we'd do our Cup Cup Foo Walk at about 20 to eight. We'd start out with eight or nine students but by the time we got back from walking around Birmingham, calling out, "Cup Cup Foo!" we'd have 30. People would just get in line and say, "This is great. This is just great."

We'd all sing, "Oh! What a Beautiful Morning," all the way through. We were the clowns of Birmingham but all these people would just fall into line. It was so much fun.

Eventually, our family moved out of Birmingham and moved to Regent Park in Troy, where I now teach. I also have a TV show on CMNTV. I've got a tremendous agent, Al Horton, who is second to none. Al has done a great job in getting our audience to where it is today, about 400,000 viewers. I've done a lot of radio shows, including Warren Pierce's show, and a lot of TV shows.

I've got a great website thanks to Jami, Jen, and Laura. I'm blessed. I'm having a ball. I just can't fathom that we're having so much fun. It's not about the money, it's about making people happy. I praise them to the hilt. We're all together. It's fun.

The thing that astounds me is hearing people say, "Oh, you're a celebrity now. I see you on TV and hear you on the radio."

I tell them, "I'm not a celebrity. I'm just Itsy."

I've had TV shows but I wasn't a star. I just touched people. I've helped people in walkers, with autism, with arthritis. I've reached out to all of them and did the best I could do to help them feel better about life. I've helped people in wheelchairs. They did the Chi exercises in their wheelchairs right along with me. I will always be there for the people who've taken my classes. If you ever want my help, contact me. Just call the number elsewhere in this book.

Chi has taught me a lot. I've grown to love helping people become what they should be. I go to the Friendship Circle and teach kids who have autism there for free. Levi Sentoff asked me to do it. The gym at the Friendship Circle is named for me. I've helped Friendship Circle for years.

In addition I go to the Jewish Home of the Aged and teach them for free because I love those people. It's not about the money, it's about giving back. Giving back is I think the most important thing in life. If you've had a big career, you could be a big shot with a big ego, but it's not the right thing to do. I've never done it.

I'm proud to say that I follow my dad, Morrie Fenkell, and Chuck Daly by making a difference in people's lives. They were all caring people who gave back to their community. I'm giving back too.

Blessed to give back

In about 2001, it was the Tuesday before Thanksgiving and I was getting ready to go to Florida for Thanksgiving. I usually go to bed early, about 9 or 9:30, because I get up early to do my exercises. I couldn't sleep so I turned on the television to watch the news. There was a report about an 84-year-old African-American lady who had been duped by two men pretending to be police officers. They went to her house and said, "Ma'am do you have any money in your safety deposit box? There's counterfeit money going around the neighborhood."

"Yes, I have $5,000 in my safety deposit box."

"Well, we have to go get it to use as evidence. We'll take the money and come back with real money."

It was a dupe and she fell for it. They emptied her safety deposit box and never came back.

I was furious! How could they do that? But you know, scams are scams.

I called Channel 2, the Fox News affiliate that ran the story. "Give me the lady's number," I said. "I want that lady's name and number right now!"

"We can't do that," they said. "We don't know who you are." They had a point. They didn't want the woman to be hurt even more than she had been.

I hung up the phone but I still couldn't sleep. The next day I called the station again. "About that lady you had that story about last night. You give her my number. Have her call me."

I went to my office as usual. In a while my secretary came in and said, "This lady wants to talk to you about what happened last night."

I grabbed the phone. It was the woman's daughter who said, "What do you want?"

"I want you to come to my office between 12 and 1 o'clock. I want you or your brother to get her here and I'm going to give your mother her money back. It was not the right thing for those guys to do. I don't want anybody to go to Thanksgiving like that."

So they came to the office and I gave them $5,000. They gave me a Christmas card, which was nice but not necessary. I'm passionate for people. I'm a practical joker, but I love people.

Lessons from the Workout Room

There are three things that I say I'm proud of:

I never drank.

I never took a drug.

I never had a fight in my life, not one, except in the dojo. Never anywhere else. I'm proud of that.

Follow what your body tells you to do. If you had a bad sleep, exercise soft. If you had a good sleep, exercise however you want. Follow what your body tells you to do. A lot of people think you have to do strenuous exercise every day. That's not the right thing to do. You follow what your body tells you to do.

If you're a runner, walk backwards for 800 yards before you start running. Why? Because the Achilles tendon, the calf and the hamstrings are the biggest casualties to athletes and when you walk backwards they get stretched.

Don't be argumentative with people. They have feelings. Treat others as you want to be treated. Don't overwork yourself to the point it becomes an obsession.

Pick the exercise that you want to do. Look at your age. Look at your body and then tell yourself what exercise you need. For example, if you can't see your feet, you are obese. Watch what you eat and do the exercises to help that.

Start each day with this salutation:

Today is the first day of the rest of your life. It's not how you look, it's how you feel. It's not what's on top of the skin that counts, it's what's under the skin that counts. Treat others as you want to be treated and don't forget you're on the right side of the dirt.

CHAPTER 4

CHAPTER
F·I·V·E

THE FAMILY ROOM

"If you live beneath your means, you will never go broke."

▶ ERWIN "ITSY" LIEBERMAN

*Itsy and Vivian's
Wedding: Sam and Ira
Lieberman*

I have a wonderful family. Let me tell you about them.

Vivian, my wife

I've been married to my wife, Vivian, for 46 years. I met her while I was at Eastern Michigan University. She was studying to be a teacher. We married while I was at Wayne State. She has been by my side for all those years. She's been a trooper.

At first, we weren't doing so well. I'd go to class at Wayne State from 8 to 11 a.m., then I'd go to work at Hampton products until 5 p.m. (My coach, Sam Marshall, got me a job there.) During the summer months, I worked at E.F. McDonald to make more money. I still did football and track. I only slept six to seven hours each night. I played football, ran track, and then I had to work. I had to help my family so I had many jobs. I was a real workhorse.

Later on, when I was in corporate America and flying in private jets, meeting celebrities, and having gourmet meals and all that, it took a lot away from my family. Vivian is the leader of our family. If you think corporate America isn't stressful, you're wrong. There is stress, depending on how big your job is. My wife stood by me all these years.

A lot of times people get pulled away and the wife has to take over. That's what my wife did and I'm so grateful.

*Sisters: Vivian, Diane,
and Bonnie*

My children

My daughter Melissa lives in Costa Mesa, California. My son Jay lives in Long Beach, California. They love California.

My daughter worked for me. My son worked for me when I was at Ha-Lo and when I had my own company. Now they are on their own. I wouldn't tell them to follow me into the industry; I wouldn't tell them not to do it. Once you're over the age of 25, you have to make your own choices. I'm proud of them.

My son calls me every day. I was so happy to have coached his teams growing up. I loved spending time with him at our cottage in Charlevoix. Years ago, we had a nice house in West Bloomfield with a creek and a woods. Jay and I would love to watch our little Puli terrorize Onyx, our German shepherd.

My daughter calls me often and she is so happy. She has a new Siberian husky and a cat. I have no grandchildren -- that's one thing I miss.

Jay's Barmitzveh

Let me tell you one funny memory I have with my daughter. Earlier I told you about meeting Steve Wynn after I lost my German shepherd Onyx. Steve had offered to send me in his private plane to Burbank, California, to pick a new dog from the breeder he used.

So when I got back home I told my daughter, who was about 25 at the time, "Melissa, it's your birthday, come with me and help me pick out my new dog."

We got into Steve Wynn's private plane and flew to Burbank. On the way there, we took in the sights. We had lunch, saw Rodeo Drive with all the exclusive boutiques where the stars shopped and so on. Melissa had a ball.

Itsy with Melissa

We went to the breeder's and we picked out Rex, a beautiful dog and we got him ready to take back home with us.

When we got back to the airport, we were told that something was wrong with the plane and we were grounded. So here I am with my daughter and this brand-new dog we know nothing about.

Jay

A lot of people were staring at us; "Oh what a beautiful dog!" But all the while we didn't know what to do. We didn't know how he'd react and we didn't know how we'd get him home. Eventually, Steve loaned us another plane, a 12 seater.

We did make it home safe and sound but what an adventure that was. How many people fly cross-country in a private plane to pick up a dog?

In my family I have great uncles and aunts and love them all. We have one solid family. We never have fights in our family and we all get along. I'm proud of that.

My second family: The Vanden Bosches

I have a lot of families. My second family, which I've just acquired over the past two years, is the Vanden Bosch family. I moved to Regent Park and we moved into a penthouse: two households on a floor. One day, I saw this guy come off the elevator. He looked like an airplane, he was bald and so muscular. I nodded to him. He nodded to me. He went to his penthouse and I went to mine and that was it.

Melissa Lieberman

"God Almighty, who was that?" I wondered. "He's got to be an athlete with that build."

I asked the management, "Who's that living in the next penthouse?"

"He's a football player but we don't want to mention the name," they said. They had strict privacy rules.

Still, I like to be neighborly, so I decided to leave my bio right outside his door. It was my way of saying, "I'm your neighbor; this is who I am."

We finally introduced ourselves in person a couple of days later. "I'm Kyle Vanden Bosch," he said. He was the new defensive end for the Detroit Lions.

I said, "I know you're new here. Anything you want, just come to me."

About two weeks later, he asked me, "Its, do you think you can get me some tickets to a Tigers game?"

Kyle Vanden Bosch with his children

"It's going to be tough, Kyle, but I think I might," I said facetiously. "How many do you need?"

"About eight," he said. "My kids are coming, my sister and

brother-in-law are coming, and my mom and dad are coming."

So I said, "I'll get them for you."

"Thanks Its."

Well I went to my friend Mike Bayoff and got them. He's the nephew of Mike Ilitch, who owns the Tigers.

I brought them to Kyle. His sister and his kids were in the car getting ready to leave for the game at Comerica Park. As I handed him the tickets, I said,

"By the way, you're throwing out the first pitch of the game."

Itsy and Vanden Bosch children

"What?!"

"You're throwing out the first pitch."

The next day, he said, "Why did you do that?"

"Because your family was there. I wanted you to do it for your family."

"Oh my God," was all he could say. From that time on, we became such good friends. One day, I said, "Kyle, I've got a new exercise for you. I'm going to teach you the Chi exercises."

"Okay. That sounds interesting." He came three times. He was supposed to come once more but didn't. "I overslept," he said.

"You didn't oversleep. Admit it -- it's too vigorous for you." (I was joking, of course – anyone can do Sunrise Chi, even a pro football player like Kyle.)

Kyle laughed and admitted, "It's too soft for me." Still, even though our exercise preferences differ, we got to be great friends, like brothers. We go everywhere together. Kyle and I are so close, I don't know if he's my big brother or I'm his little brother. His kids call Vivian and me "Grandma and Grandpa from the East." I call them the Bandits. They are magnificent: He has Payton, Case, and Bastien.

Kyle and I watch each other's backs. When he goes out of town, I get the mail. When I go out of town, he does the same. He's one of the nicest guys I know. His mom and dad and family are super. Whenever we get together we have a great time. I have the utmost respect for him. He's now dating a beautiful girl named Steph. She's very astute.

I should also mention that Kyle was a 4.0 student in four years in high school, All American in football. If you want a guy to be a president or general manager of your team, it's Kyle Vanden Bosch.

Kyle's Brother-In-Law, Amy, Stephanie, Vivian and Itsy

I will tell you right now, America, you find me a leader that is better than Kyle Vanden Bosch. I'll bet you can't. The Detroit Lions' Coach Jim Schwartz made him the captain of the Lions and he could not have made a better choice. In two years, Kyle's taken them from two wins to six wins to 10 wins. Why? Because he's the leader of the team. I will bet anyone that there's not a better leader than he is.

I've got to tell one story about Kyle. I was in the apartment and Kyle came walking down the hall, with Steph. He was wearing only shorts, no shirt, to show off his muscles.

I backed away in mock horror.

President Obama and Mr. & Mrs. Willie Horton

"Steph! Get that brute away from me," I said jokingly. "I am afraid of that guy... Ooh! Get him away from me!"

"Itsy! He's a cupcake," Steph said.

So now we call him Cupcake. Because he's the sweetest guy you'd ever want to know. But don't get him mad.

My third family: The Hortons

Now we go to another one of my families: The Horton family. People in Detroit remember Willie from his days with the Detroit Tigers. He was on the championship team in '68. Willie and Gloria Horton are saints, wonderful people. I'm Willie's go-to guy. Anytime he wants something, I'll help him the best I can. Gloria is lucky and Willie's lucky because they've been married so many years. The Hortons all get along. I'm invited to all their parties. We have a lot of fun. Willie is such a gracious guy. He'll do anything for charity. His son Al is my agent and he's so astute and so gracious. He has a wonderful wife in Jody and they have three girls. I'm proud to be part of their family and they are a part of mine.

My fourth family: The Versacis

The Versaci family is another one of my families. Tony is head of the Michigan Sports All-State team every year. He was the third best football coach in the state of Michigan. He coached at Divine Child. He's partners with Mike Lucci in Burger King franchises.

My wife is very close to Tony's wife, Sally. Vivian and I have gone on a lot of trips with Tony and Sally, including three trips to Italy and two cruises. They have the most beautiful two daughters. Their son Mike owns a wonderful restaurant and their son-in-law Pete is a great doctor. They are wonderful to be around. Their kids are very smart.

More family:

Chuck Daly

Now I think we should go to Chuck Daly. We'll start by saying I'm dedicating this book to Chuck Daly and Morrie Fenkell and Sam Young (he was my best friend).

I met Chuck through Frank Gallagher. Frank's roommate was Billy Cunningham, Chuck's main man. If Billy was the class of class, then Chuck was the class of class of class. I met Chuck and we became friends. We used to go to dinner almost every week when we were in Michigan -- Chuck and Terry and me and my wife.

Chuck Daley's 75th Birthday

When I went to Ballenisles in Florida, Chuck went to Jupiter Hills, which was nearby, so we'd go out there too. We'd play golf with Billy, Rollie, and all those guys. I was so close to Chuck, when Cydney, his daughter, got married in North Carolina, I was happy to be able to help them. It happened like this:

One day Chuck called me. "Its, I've got a problem," he said.

"What is it?"

"Cydney's husband isn't working now and neither is she," Chuck said. "Do you know anyone in Carolina?"

Well I was president of Ha-Lo in Michigan and I was their top producer. I said, "I think I can help her."

I got her a job in North Carolina. She worked there for six, seven years. The company didn't like it because she didn't really know anything about the job at first but she stayed on and did great. They eventually moved to Wisconsin when her husband got a job there. I went to their daughter Sabrina's christening. I went to their son Connor's christening in Wisconsin. We traveled there with Chuck and it was great.

When we went to Wisconsin for Connor's christening. Chuck said, "Its, this is a Catholic church we're going to."

"What are you getting at?"

"Well we've got to wear a suit or sport coat."

We both wore suits. Well, "Daddy Wags," as we called him, showed up with all his Beau Brummell attire. We walked into the church and there was not one other guy with a tie on in the whole church. We really stood out.

"You set me up," I fumed at him.

"Well, I didn't know."

"No, you just wanted to show off your clothes." He laughed his socks off. That's how Chuck and I were. He'd tell me things. I'd tell him things.

We'd play golf with Billy. It was great relationship. I'm still close with his wife, Terry. Vivian will go shopping with her and to lunch, because we're all so close. I talk to Cydney often.

Chuck and I would always go to lunch together. One day, Chuck said, "How did you make so much money in corporate America?"

"Why'd you ask me that question?"

"I know you were very successful. How did you do it?" He had just gotten out of basketball at that time.

I told him, "I ride the wave."

"What do you mean by that?"

"If the wave gets wavy, I ride it. If it calms down, I calm down. I do what I have to do and don't get in anybody's way and don't get involved in any controversy. I just ride the wave."

And he said to me, "That's what I do."

"What do you mean?"

He said, "Its, do you believe I'm going to discipline these guys? They're getting paid five times what I'm getting paid. I ride the wave like you said, but not in that manner, because I get paid to win."

"That's what I got paid to do, win," I said.

"So what I do: I tell them who's starting. I tell them who's going to play and the game plan. I had a captain. The captain I told what to do and he'd come to me and say, 'I told this guy this and that guy that, like you said.'"

I said "That's what I did when I was coaching. I had a captain and I said 'You do this. If you can't do it, I'll have to get involved.'"

Chuck said. "Then I put on my suit and go out and I'll be Daddy Wags and put on a show. I never had a curfew because I didn't want a curfew. I didn't want to go in their room and see what was in their rooms. They should be mature enough to handle their own lives without me telling them how to do it. Bill Davidson said to me, 'I want to win.'" And that's what I'm going to do."

"Well, you know Chuck," I said. "I did the same thing."

We just laughed at each other. We told each other, "Holy

crap!" Our minds were joined together. He worked through his pressures and I worked through mine and we were successful.

When Chuck passed away, we had about a half-mile or so to walk to the cemetery. A car pulled up next to me – it was Pat Riley, longtime coach of the Miami Heat.

"Hi, I'm Itsy."

"Oh, you're Itsy? Chuck always talked about you!"

"Thank you, Pat," I said. "That means a lot."

"Itsy, when we were coaches, I hated Chuck Daley. He always beat me or I always beat him. He always dressed better than I did. Or I would dress better than he did. We were always the showboats of the game. He had the Bad Boys. I had the Show Times. We hated each other. When he retired and we got to be friends, I grew to love him. I'm going to miss him dearly."

Chuck, we miss you 100 percent, your family, your children and your friends. Be proud that this book is dedicated to you with love and devotion.

I was there for Chuck's 75th birthday, and all the guys were there: Billy Cunningham, Joe Dumars, Vinnie Johnson, and all of them. I don't know if Detroit knows this but the Bad Boys were the pallbearers for Chuck Daly.

I miss Chuck every single day.

Our family's savior: Morrie Fenkell

How can I say it other than this? I owe everything to Morrie Fenkell. He was our savior.

Morrie was my first cousin and owned a packing house. My dad was a Damon Runyon character, always getting in and out of trouble. We went bankrupt twice. If it wasn't for Morrie

Fenkell stepping in every time we needed it, we never would have been the family we were. He was a gentleman's gentleman. He dressed very, very neat but not ostentatiously. He was always very gracious, with impeccable manners. He'd always say, "Thank you so much for doing this," no matter what the thing was.

Godsons Michael and Robert Young

In later years, Morrie bought Liberty State Bank. He was president and he sat in a chair up in the front. He didn't want an office in the back because he was a commoner. He wasn't a showboat. Everybody who knew him just raved about him. He was a founder and board member of Huntington Bank.

The reason why my dad's Raleigh House was successful is because Morrie is the one who gave Dad the money. Then he got nine other people to put money in. Why? Because they trusted him. Everybody that knew him, trusted Morrie Fenkell.

Morrie and his wife, Sybil, were nice people. You'd never know they were multimillionaires. They never acted that way. They raised their son Steve that way, too. I love spending time with Steve and Bobbie and their kids.

I've always been grateful for what Morrie did for us but didn't have a tangible way to show it until the 1980s. In 1982, I was doing very well – we had General Motors and Chrysler so I was making a very nice living. But my dad passed away that year and left me with a very bad dilemma --$350,000 of debt. Keep in mind that this was in 1982, during the Carter administration, when the economy was going bad.

The way I saw it, I had three choices:

1. I could go bankrupt and tell the bank, owned by my cousin who had already done so much, "I can't pay it."
2. Ask my cousin to loan or give me $350,000.
3. Pay it off. I didn't have that kind of money, but I could at least try.

I loved my dad very much. I didn't want my dad's legacy to be a mountain of debts. It'd be like he had broken his word to Morrie.

I asked Morrie for a meeting with him and Ken Kazusky, his loan officer. I sat down with them and said, "I'm going to pay the loan back. I'm shooting for $70,000 a year for five years."

"That's a tremendous thing you're offering to do," Morrie said.

"You've been great to me. I can't let you down," I said. "I'll work my ass off to see that it's paid off. What's more, I'm going to pay the interest, too."

Well, I'm a Lieberman and I worked my buns off. I'd run to Pontiac in the morning, then to Chrysler in the afternoon. And I'd entertain the big wigs in the evening.

Vivian's Parents

I was so focused on Morrie and on keeping my family afloat that I paid off the loan in three years.

Morrie and Ken were so impressed, they wanted to go to the Detroit Free Press and have them do an article about it, showing that people could still meet their financial obligations if they worked hard. I wouldn't let them. I did it for family – for Morrie.

I can't say enough about my cousin. Thank you Morrie for keeping our house in order and for loving my dad and mom so much. I hope you and my dad and Chuck Daly and Sam Young will look down and be happy that this book has been written.

Italian family: Jerry Vitale

Another person I will always have a great deal of affection for is Jerry Vitale. He took over the Machus Red Fox restaurant (the last place Jimmy Hoffa was seen alive) when it failed several years after Hoffa's disappearance. Jerry owned a restaurant in Grand Blanc, which closed when the economy went bad in the 1980s. His brother Tom and Joe Vicari started the Andiamo chain of restaurants.

"Itsy, I've got a great thing," Jerry said. "Tom and Joe gave me a percentage to run the Andiamo's Restaurant in West Bloomfield. Would you be interested in splitting it with me? You'd put up the money and I'll run it."

I said, "Jerry, I'm sorry, but I'm not going to do it because of one reason. We've been friends for so long and I love you but it just wouldn't work out. But what I will do is guarantee a loan for you. You make the payments but if anything goes wrong, I'll be liable for it. I trust you."

What eventually happened was he paid off the loan and eventually ran six Andiamo's restaurants. Jerry never forgot that and whenever we meet, we embrace.

Andiamo's is going strong and I am so happy for them all. In life, you sometimes have to step in

Jerry and Tommy Vitale, Jimmy Derron, and Itsy

and help other people who need it. I've had many second chances and that's why I give second chances to others. I know what it is to have to claw your way up from the bottom.

I think the reason he asked me, besides our friendship, was because of the way Italians and Jews do so well in business partnerships. I have a great respect for Italians, as you can see from my story, and I've known quite a few: Jack Gilardi, Jerry Vitale, and Tony (who owns the Papa Joes markets), classy Gary D'Alessandro, talented Mike Chirco, likeable Mike Lucci and Lou Comaianni. These are just a few of them.

Childhood family: Sam Young

Sam Young and I met when we were three years old in Detroit. We were best friends for more than 45 years. We played slow-pitch together. He had a football scholarship to Southern Cal. I had a few of them, but he was a much better player than I was. He was always so nonchalant, so easygoing. He raised two beautiful kids in Mike and Robbie. He was in the senior World Racquetball championships. He was the best man at my wedding. I was the best man at his wedding. We had a ton of fun. I used to play too many practical jokes on him.

The day Sam died I just fell apart. But as things go, his two sons are my godsons. I watch over them. They will never have any need of anything and they know that. We keep in touch. They're super people. I've known his wife Gail for a ton of years. She's doing well but I know she misses him terribly.

Sam, when you're looking down and reading this book, I want to remind you that in all the time that we played softball together, you were the only one who never slid. And you're the only guy who tagged out on a ground ball. He never got his pants dirty, never in 200 to 300 games. He was a power hitter and a lefty but he never, ever slid. Never.

Family in high places: Jack Gilardi

Jack was one of my best friends through the years and certainly the most powerful. He's one of the real movers and shakers in Hollywood and I met him in the most innocuous way possible.

I was waiting in line in a hotel in Phoenix in 1987 where I was attending a celebrity golf outing. I had taken along Mel Goulsin. Mel had gotten a big order at Chrysler for us and I wanted to reward him for it. Anyway, I was in line at the registration desk when I heard a voice behind me:

"Wow! Where did you get such a beautiful bag? That's beautiful leather!"

I was carrying a leather carry-on bag with the Super Bowl insignia.

"Well, I'm in marketing," I told the man, "We gave 500 of these to Ford dealers as a room gift. Do you want one?"

"I'd love one," he said. "My name's Jack Gilardi."

"Jack, you've got it," I said. "I'm Itsy Lieberman."

The two of us, and the actor Mike Connors, spent a lot of time together at the golf tournament so by the end of the five days, we were pretty good friends. It was one heck of a tournament – I played with Susan Anton. (We were the Mutt and Jeff team – I was 5 foot 6 and she was 5 foot 11.)

During the course of the tournament, I found out that Jack had three kids. After I got back home, I sent four of the Super Bowl bags to him, one for each of his kids and one to share with his wife, Annette Funicello, the former Musketeer. That impressed him and he called me as soon as he got them.

"My God, I'm so glad to meet a guy of your character," he said. "It's amazing that someone would do that for my kids."

We became so close, we were pretty much a partnership. I'd call him, "Jack, can you get a star to help us with this launch?" I'd ask. Or he'd say, "Its, can you help out Howie Long? He's trying to break into acting?"

We'd talk every week. I went to all the weddings for his three children, Jackie, Gina, and Jason. I'd go to California to visit him two or three times a year.

One day I got call from Jack's assistant.

"Itsy, Jack wants to talk to you," he said in his usual gruff voice, sounding like a gangster.

Soon Jack is on the line, "Its! I've been chosen Man of the Year for the Race for the Cure. They're having a gala at Paramount Studios for me, 2,700 people will be there. I want you and Vivian to come."

"Schmekel (my nickname for him)!" I said. "You know I'll be there."

Vivian and I flew out to California with her sister and brother-in-law. The night before the festivities, Jack hosted a party for us at his house with a lot of his friends, including some big name stars.

Then the day of the awards dinner came. We could not believe it – there was anything you could want to eat, including steak. There were bands playing, you name it. We sat with Frankie Avalon, John Saxon, and Jimmy Darren.

Jack was walking around like Jack does. We saw Charlton Heston, Sylvester Stallone, Jaclyn Smith, Samuel L. Jackson – all there to honor my friend Jack.

When the festivities started, the master of ceremonies said, "We're here to honor Jack Gilardi, the Icon of Icons."

Well, a lot of people got up to pay tribute and we all stood up when Jack himself took the stage. So he's up there, talking and talking and talking, when suddenly I hear him say:

"I want everybody to know that one of my best friends flew from Detroit to California to honor me. I want Itsy and Vivian Lieberman to stand up."

I almost flipped. I didn't want to do a speech. I didn't know what to do.

We stood up and Jack said, "Itsy, I love you." I was stunned. I sat down and looked at Frankie Avalon in shock.

All I could think was, "Boy oh boy! He throws a party for us on Friday. Then on Saturday, he has me stand up with my wife at a banquet. Charlton Heston! Samuel L. Jackson! And Itsy Lieberman?!

Oy Gevalt!

But that's how Jack is. That's how close we are.

While we were in California, Jack told us he wanted us to see "what Hollywood is really like". We went to Ago, the restaurant owned by Robert DeNiro.

There were more "10s" than you could shake a stick at. We saw all the wannabees. The women were beautiful. The men were all tanned and muscular. And all of them were going up to Jack, fawning all over him. "Jack, Is there anything coming up for me?" "Jack, I'd really like to be in that movie." One beautiful woman came up to him and cooed, "Jack is there anything I can do for you?" He is the most magnetic, charismatic guy you'll ever meet in your life.

I've got a funny story that shows how much power Jack has.

I went to California with my agent, Al Horton. While we were there, I told him, "I want you to meet this man. We'll go to Jack's office."

We went to his office at International Creative Management (ICM), where Jack is the executive vice president. His assistant Justin meets us and lets us know we have 45 minutes to meet with Jack. We go in, and it's all "Schmekel!" "Itsy!" I introduce Al and we get to chatting.

Jack's office was like a museum; he's got all sorts of sports and Hollywood memorabilia, stuff from DiMaggio, Pacino, and Stallone. He's the original Godfather.

Justin comes in, "Jack! Shirley MacLaine is on the phone. She says it's an emergency. She has to talk to you right now!"

Jack tells Justin, "Tell her I'll call her in an hour. Itsy's here."

I look at Al, who happens to be African-American. At that moment his face almost turned to Caucasian: Imagine someone telling a star like Shirley MacLaine to call back just because of me!

What's more, we stayed another hour and when we left there was another guy waiting to see Jack. I didn't know who he was but I could tell from his clothes and his demeanor that he was somebody important.

Yet, I'm not better than anyone. That's just the kind of guy Jack is. I'm blessed to have a friend like that. I'd do anything to help him or his family.

When we went to dinner with his whole family, we had a private room at the restaurant and we laughed for three hours straight! I picked up the bill. I beat him to it because he's such a great guy I wanted to be the best host I can for him.

CHAPTER 5

Football family: Joe Schmidt

Another of my best friends is Joe Schmidt, the face of the Detroit Lions.

I've known Joe since 1964 or '65. Frank Gallagher introduced me and we all used to go to the Bellanger House in Royal Oak – me, Frank, Joe, and Bill Munson.

If you want two words to describe Joe they're "gentleman" and "class." On the football field, you don't mess with him. A lot of people, when they hear the name "Detroit Lions," they think of Barry Sanders. Not me – I think of Joe. He was All Pro, he coached for two or three yeas and had the best record for five years.

Joe Schmidt and I often go to BallinIsles to play nine holes. We don't keep score, we just have fun. He and Marilyn and Vivian and I go to dinner often. It's such an honor to know them.

To show you what kind of a person he is: Alex Webster, the fullback for the New York Giants, is now in a wheelchair. One day, my friend Jerry Faccianio asked me to get Joe to come to his house for the Super Bowl, saying Alex would be there and would love to meet Joe. And Joe did. He could have gone anywhere, but he went to be with Alex. I'd say that's the mark of the best football player. No disrespect meant for Barry Sanders but Joe Schmidt is the best, hands down.

Life lessons from the family room

Have great friends and love them to death.

Always be beside people who love you and you show your love for them.

Humor and remembrances live forever.

Vivian, Jay, Melissa, and Onyx

Epilogue

If there's one thing I want people to know about my life, it's that I'm passionate about people.

Whether I was coaching, marketing, or teaching, I always said, "Put a smile on your face. Feel good about yourself."

I don't want to stop now. In fact, I have an idea that maybe you, my readers, can help me with.

I used to watch the Jerry Lewis Telethon for Muscular Dystrophy every Labor Day weekend. Did you know he raised $2.4 billion over the years? That's a tremendous thing. Jerry brought on a lot of celebrities who did their thing and helped bring in a lot of money to help others.

Jerry Lewis is no longer with the Telethon: he's in his 80s and has his share of health problems, as we all do. But nobody does telethons anymore and that's a shame.

If I ever get the chance, I would love to get sponsors and do something similar. I'd get the pharmaceutical companies and the home medical equipment companies and we'd raise money to help people. I believe in this so much, that I'd put in some of my own money to do it.

When I had my own show in the '80s, I showed that I could teach Sunrise Chi to people in wheelchairs and walkers. I taught people with muscular dystrophy, polio, and arthritis. I really helped them and I'd like to bring it back so I can help more.

If I could, I'd bring in celebrities and athletes and have a new telethon. We could have a day for people who are disabled or disadvantaged. We could call it "Feel Good Day." While I've met a lot of celebrities, I'm afraid a lot of them would get huffy and ask, "How much will I get paid?"

My answer to that would be, "You can sing. These people can't. You can run. They can't even stand up. Have a little humility and give back to those who don't have anything."

That's what I'd like to do. If any of you want to help me make that happen, call me, or my agent Al Horton. (The information is elsewhere in this book.)

Conclusion

Well, you've read to the last page. I hope you've enjoyed reading it as much as I have enjoyed telling it.

Mom and dad, wherever you are in heaven, I hope you're looking down and are proud of your only child. You're my flesh and blood and you mean more to me than anything. I hope as you look down, you say, "That's my beautiful son."

I dedicated this book to Morrie and Chuck as well because you each have a well-deserved place in heaven. I hope all five of us will get together when I meet you all in heaven because if it wasn't for you, this book would never have been written.

In loving memory, I want to recognize George Cantor, a great writer/sports commentator in the Detroit area. He's the one who encouraged me to write this book. "You've accomplished so much," he said.

George published many books about athletes and others from all walks of life. He was a great friend. He would have written this book but he passed much too soon. George, I hope you are looking down and enjoying this book. Please know that Vivian and I are taking good care of Sherry.

Thanks

I want to thank all the people who have helped me in my career. You've helped me and my family live a very nice life. To you suppliers and those in the Big Three, I hope you will say, "Itsy, thank you for bringing me all those programs, for helping with all those launches and all those incentives. You were always there when we needed you. Four people who especially helped me at Ford were Jim Gwaltney, Steve Lyons, Jim O'Connor, and Daryl Hazel.

Thank you for making me a lot of money. But I don't need it; yesterday I found my bar mitzvah money!

I've always given credit where credit is due. Even though my name is on the cover of this book, I didn't do it alone. So, my deepest thanks go to:

Al Horton, my agent, the best ever. I wouldn't know how to have done this without him.

Laura Brestovansky, my writer. She wrote this book. I spoke and she put my words into something readable. She deserves a lot of credit.

Thanks also to Scott Frush, who inspired me to finally write this book and also saw it through the production phase. He's also my financial advisor and has done so much for me.

Jami Fresch, Jen Fresard, and Laura are my website developers. What a wonderful job they did with the site. I didn't even have to do that much with it because I am so confident in their abilities. They are doing a great job.

I would also like to give credit and thanks to Les Gorback of Gorback Studio of Photography for the wonderful cover photo of me. Terrific work!

And last but not least:

To my wife, for not sticking her nose in my business. Vivian

has always let me do what I wanted. She never criticized what I did. She just went with the flow, supporting me in all my efforts. I appreciate her so much.

From the Heart of Itsy

I hope you liked the book – the humor and the stories. Even though it's called, "Sixty Years Young with Itsy', the book isn't about me.

I was fortunate to have been at the right place at the right time with the right people -- the people this book is about.

Usually when a book or movie or play comes out, the author comes out to take a bow. I'm not going to do that. Instead I want my family, friends, and all the other people who were there with me to take that bow.

Just remember, you'll never beat Nick Mondella or me in the Red Zone.

Good day,

Itsy

About the Author

Erwin "Itsy" Lieberman lives in Troy, Michigan, with his wife of 46 years, Vivian. After successful careers in coaching and in marketing, he enjoys making a difference by teaching Sunrise Chi on television and at various locations in Metro Detroit.

About the Co-Author

Laura Brestovansky is a freelance writer based in Michigan. Her byline has appeared in many publications, including the *Oakland Press* and the *Michigan Catholic*. She has also ghostwritten several non-fiction books.